S

# Sedated

*The Secret That Everybody Knew —*
*One Family's Struggle with Addiction*

## Britt Doyle

PRECOCITY PRESS

This is a work of nonfiction. It reflects the author's present recollections of experiences in the past.

Editor: Ruth Mullen
Creative Director: Susan Shankin
Cover design: Patti McMahon
Cover image: Truth Doyle
Portrait of Wynne Doyle: Mark Stock

Text set in Baskerville

Library of Congress Control Number is available.

Because of the dynamic nature of the Internet, any Web addresses or links contained in this book may have changed since publication and may no longer be valid.

Permission from Shatterproof to use their two-page document has been granted.

ISBN: 978-0-9987963-0-7

Published by Precocity Press
612 Santa Clara Avenue, Venice, CA 90291
www.precocitypress.com


First edition. Printed and bound in the United States of America

*I dedicate this book to Truth,*
*who has shown up every day, whether it*
*was to encourage or to pick up the pieces;*
*to Preston, Harry, and Little Britt,*
*for being strong and willing to communicate*
*not only with me but with anyone*
*who will listen; and to Julian, who has had*
*to share his mother with the rest of us.*

We dance round in a ring and suppose,
but the secret sits in the middle and knows.

— ROBERT FROST, *The Secret Sits*

# Contents

1. It Wasn't Supposed to Be Like This          1

2. A Happy Start          11

3. Babies on the Way          19

4. The Holiday that Wasn't          27

5. Seeking Help          39

6. Relapse          49

7. The Big Picture          57

8. A Change of Scenery to Break the Cycle          63

9. If You're Not Part of the Solution          71

10. Falling Apart          81

11. Desperation and Anger          91

12. Permission                              107

13. Upheaval                                115

14. Taking Control                          129

15. Financial Ruin                          149

16. Coming Back to Life                     157

17. Overdose                                167

18. Helping Others                          175

19. Through the Eyes of the Children        185

    Life Lessons                            193

    Acknowledgements                        195

    Bibliography                            197

    Resources                               201

    About the Author                        209

# Chapter 1

# It Wasn't Supposed to Be Like This

## I AM THE BEAUTIFUL

*I am the beautiful, quiet Mill Valley.*
*The pale pink house on the ocean shore.*
*The big golden labradoodle with the mile-long smile.*

*I am also the white house on Russian Hill with unlimited stairs*
*    leading up to the doorway.*
*The cable cars that roll past, and a view that takes your breath*
*    away.*
*I am two different worlds, connected together by one bridge.*

*I am keeping my feelings inside until I finally burst.*
*I am getting through my family problems.*
*I am the girl who is somehow always caught in the middle.*
*Just trying to find my way out.*
*I am trying to get over my past, so I can begin a new future.*

*I am not just small and weak like you all may think.*
*I am not just sensitive and girly.*
*I am more than this.*
*I am strong and brave.*
*I am calm and relaxed, and find the best in people.*
*I am humble and kind.*
*I show love and care towards my friends and family.*

*I am a warm summer day.*
*I am taking thousands of pictures.*
*I am dancing on rooftops, listening to loud music.*
*I am the sound of laughter and the feel of excitement.*
*Above all, I am me.*

—K. BRITT DOYLE (Little Britt), age nine

"DAD? I DON'T think we'll be able to make the Easter party this morning at the club. Mom's dead." Harry's voice was monotone, numb. I could hear Preston in the background, still screaming to the 911 operator on the other end of the phone line that his mother was dead. My daughter Britt had stayed overnight with my wife Truth and me, which meant her brothers—mere teenagers themselves—were having to deal with this on their own. A shot of adrenaline coursed through my body as the weight of what was happening came down like a dark curtain. I ran into the bedroom where Britt was sleeping. I'll never forget the look on her face as I explained to her that her mother had passed away. She was in total shock. I could hardly believe it myself. But deep down, I had been expecting this day for a long time.

Wynne, the mother of my children, passed away during the night on Saturday, March 21, 2015, at the age of fifty-two, after a long battle with alcohol and prescription drugs. She had been a beautiful, vibrant woman when we first met, twenty-two years earlier. We married in 1995, and had three children over the next five years. Wynne continued to dazzle as a marathon runner and world traveler. She was a devoted aunt to her several young nieces who looked up to her because she genuinely cared. But by the time she died, her substance abuse had affected everything—from our marriage and our family to my career.

Postpartum depression followed Britt's birth—Wynne's third by cesarean section—in 2000. Wynne's doctor prescribed medication to ease her pain, and that was the spark that led to what ultimately became a debilitating addiction. By Christmas of that same year, Wynne was already in rehab at her first treatment center. Less than fifteen years later, she would be dead. But in 2000, postpartum depression and drug addiction were not topics either of us talked about. We weren't alone in this; no one at the time discussed the dangers openly. The Internet was not the information source it is now, so we relied on the various doctors we saw and the medication regimens they ordered. It wasn't until Andrea Yates drowned her five children in 2001 that the world began to take postpartum depression seriously, and it wasn't until around that same time that people began to see a rapidly developing crisis stemming from the massive increase in opioid dependence and addiction in our country.

According to the Center for Disease Control, opioid-related deaths have increased by 200 percent since 2000 in the United States. Many of the victims, like Wynne, received their first exposure to opioids in a hospital setting. The National Institute of Health's Institute on Drug Abuse finds that today more than four out of five young heroin addicts started out using prescription opiates. Wynne drew the line at "street drugs." She never would have tried heroin because above all else she was a lady. On the other hand, she didn't have to face that choice, because she found plenty of doctors willing to prescribe the pain relievers she craved. I can't tell you how many times I heard the phrase "I'm just following the doctor's orders!"

I believe that the numerous stints in rehab facilities had no effect on her because she never once considered herself an "addict." She never thought she had anything whatsoever in common with the other people she shared "28 days" with because in her mind, she was just doing what the doctor ordered her to do. The internal struggle must have torn her apart. That is why standard substance abuse treatment never worked.

I'm writing this book not to expose or hurt anyone mentioned, but to tell a story of what can happen when addiction rips through a family. Perhaps these words can shed some light on the human side of addiction and help other families who are facing these same struggles. I don't blame Wynne, because addiction is a disease, not a choice. The story is immensely tragic, and touches so many lives. My family learned far more about the effects of addiction on individuals and their families than anyone would ever want to know. I'm incredibly angry at a medical and psychological community that with all of the technological tools it has at its disposal, still allows this epidemic to exist, and in some cases seemingly drives it. Societal norms that encourage silence have also contributed to and in many cases accelerated the problem.

———

"I'm sorry, sir, but we can't discuss your wife's account due to HIPAA regulations," said the pharmacist at Walgreens during one of many visits I made in 2005.

"I know that," I replied. "I'm not looking to *discuss* anything. I'm here to *tell* you something. You need to know that you're not the only one filling prescriptions for her. She's getting the same medication from several different doctors and none of you are communicating with one another! *Please* stop filling the prescriptions!"

I made calls to the doctors each time I found a new prescription bottle somewhere in the house.

"I don't want to see your name on another pill bottle in my house . . . EVER!" I screamed into the phone to one particular doctor who seemed to refill bottles almost weekly from what I found.

"Are you threatening me?" he stuttered.

"You bet I am! If I find another bottle with your name on it, I swear I'll come down to your office with a baseball bat." I was shaking.

I became manic about trying to find pills and bottles of alcohol hidden around the house before Wynne could consume them. I couldn't keep up. They were hidden in her shoes, between the mattresses, in the pockets of the coats hanging in her closet—even inside the container of rice in the pantry. My desperate need to find and dispose of any substance she could abuse was completely taking over my life. By 2005, she had already been in the emergency room several times for overdosing. After spending a night or two in the hospital, she'd attend a treatment program at an addiction facility. But she didn't receive the tools and help she needed and sooner or later she relapsed. It was the same pattern every time. She was angry, and so was I. This wasn't supposed to be the way we were going to live our lives. This wasn't the way we were going to raise our kids.

"We are not going to be a statistic!" I would remind Wynne on various occasions. "We will beat this."

But in the end, she could not free herself from the treacherous grip of addiction. I think the shame, embarrassment, humiliation, and guilt she felt must have been overwhelming to face, which made her even angrier with me and the situation in which we found ourselves.

·

The funeral was painful on so many levels. Most obvious was the realization on the part of everyone present of the void she left in her children's lives. They had lost their mother. Britt, the youngest of our three teenagers, read a weighty poem with her brothers standing at her side.

The stories and memories that Wynne's family and friends shared made the loss that much worse. Wynne had lived such a rich and full life. She had climbed to Base Camp on Mount Everest. She had worked with Hindu women in Ladakh, a town near the foot of the Himalayas, where she met His Holiness the Dalai Lama. She had acquired an extensive knowledge of India, where she spent many weeks over her lifetime.

I, on the other hand, was not part of the funeral in any way. During the service, no reference was made to our marriage and our years together as husband and wife. No one spoke of me as the father of her children. I was conspicuously edited out of the video of her life that her parents had prepared. In the eyes of her family, I was to blame for Wynne's addictive illness.

Most notable to me at the funeral was the fact that so many of our friends—as well as many of her friends from before she met me—were not there. They had failed to stay in her life over the last decade, which is so common in addiction scenarios. People finally give up on the addict. They feel they have to, to save themselves.

# Chapter 2

# A Happy Start

*Acknowledgement is the first step to recovery—*
*for everyone in the family. You can't help people*
*who don't want to help themselves.*

WYNNE KATHERINE HUTCHINS was born to upper-class parents in Orinda, California, on November 22, 1962. Her father owned a chemical company where Wynne would work as an event planner after college and before she had kids. She went to Miramonte High School, where she was a cheerleader and homecoming queen, and then studied at the University of Southern California in Los Angeles.

Wynne's parents were stoic and reserved. That's how their generation was brought up, and that, in turn, was how they raised Wynne, her two brothers, and her sister. The children were taught that you do not air your dirty laundry; you do not talk about private issues in public.

If you have a problem, you deal with it; be strong. Although there is definitely some value to that way of thinking, we now know that holding things in and suffering alone doesn't work in the long run. I believe that one of the reasons Wynne couldn't get past her addiction is that she couldn't even admit to it, much less talk about it openly. She hid her struggle as much as possible, and that kept her from fully connecting with those around her. She lived in a prison of her own making and it ultimately killed her. She never learned how to ask for help, nor to forgive herself for not being able to.

I first met Wynne in 1993, when I was twenty-eight years old and she was thirty-two. Her grace and elegance were offset by a certain awkward confidence that I found endearing. She was sarcastic and funny, with a sharp tongue and a temper that could flash without warning. I used to kid her that she had been a trucker in a past life. Her friends and relatives told me she was always the one who everyone made sure was taken care of no matter what, though. She also had a soft, sweet side that became increasingly masked over the years by the effort required to cover up her massive secret. At the beginning of our relationship, we were constantly out and about in the trendiest San Francisco restaurants, Wynne always impeccably dressed and looking gorgeous. Her long dark hair swirled around her beautiful face as if she were perpetually in a wind machine, and with her 5'7", 125-pound frame, she looked just as incredible in jeans as in the designer suits she tended to prefer.

I was introduced to Wynne by my co-worker, David. David knew Wynne through his wife at the time, who had been one of Wynne's best friends growing up. When we met, I was available—it had been a year or so since my last long-term relationship had dissolved. Wynne, however, had a boyfriend.

That was okay, because I was definitely not looking for a relationship. I was focused on trying to build my wealth management practice. But Wynne was a welcome distraction to the long days that for the most part began at 4:30 in the morning, and ended with a dinner out with clients or friends. It wasn't long after we met that she began introducing me to her single girlfriends. I think we both realized that wasn't the right way to go after it became apparent Wynne was going to either be a third wheel on the "date" or it would be a double date (which only happened once). We always seemed to have the most in common, at times leaving the others at the table out of the conversation.

A few months after we met, my firm awarded me a one-week trip to Mexico for hitting certain performance goals. Wynne accepted my invitation, and we were off. I think the moment I knew we were meant to be together came when we decided to go for a midnight swim in the ocean—and we lost our clothes to the waves! Running and hiding behind trees and cabanas until we could reach the towel station near the outdoor pool was as much fun as I had had in years. Wynne had no fear. We ended up wrapping ourselves in too-small towels to make the final journey through the lobby and up the elevators. There were four hundred other Merrill Lynch employees from the West Coast at that hotel, and our story made it through the ranks pretty quickly. Indeed, a very proud moment!

One of my best friends and I used to talk about the attributes of a woman that we thought would make the ideal wife. Among the many traits we outlined, we decided that a woman who grew up with a brother and had a loving, respectful relationship with her father was a must. We reasoned that because men can be difficult to live with, a woman who had already experienced living with men would enter a relationship already running. Not only did Wynne have two older brothers (and a sister), she would glow when she told stories about growing up with her father. Her childhood was filled with raft trips, camping trips, hiking trips, mountain climbing, and marathons that the two of them would train for together. The stories were endless, and I was completely in awe. Although I grew up in a loving family, too—my father was by my side all the way as I struggled in high school to attain my Eagle Scout rank in Boy Scouts, and nobody could have been prouder when I became captain of the tennis team and the cross country team as well—Wynne's relationship with her father seemed to be on another level. It was intoxicating the closer I got to her family.

*"Sir? Sir?" I said loudly as I followed him out the door. He kept walking, dismissively. I'm sure there had been many other men in Wynne's life who had tried to get to know her parents. She was a very attractive woman, after all.*

*"Please, Mr. Hutchins?" I said again, loudly. "I need to ask you a question."*

*He turned around and actually managed to keep walking toward his car as he appeared to listen.*

*I blurted it out. "I was hoping to talk to you about marrying your daughter."*

*This time he stopped short with a giant grin on his face.*

*"Wow! Okay. Let's set up a breakfast next week in the city," he exclaimed. "What do I get out of this deal?" he added jokingly. "I'd like a new fly rod. How about that?"*

---

I knew he was kidding, but just the same, I showed up with a new fly fishing rod, just to play it safe. Her father and I met for breakfast at the Carnelian Room, an elegant restaurant with breathtaking views located at the top of the Bank of America building in San Francisco, so that I could show respect by formally requesting his daughter's hand in marriage. Wynne had warned me that her dad would ask all kinds of deeply personal questions. That was okay with me. I had nothing to hide, and I was proud of who I was, for sure. Why wouldn't he be, as well? It was during that breakfast that he suggested that we should go fishing in the Alaskan wilderness with his two sons. It was a trip that allowed us to get to know each other with no other distractions. It was perfect.

In fact, everything was perfect. My job was fulfilling and I worked with terrifically smart people; I was in great shape; I had met an amazing woman who was not only gorgeous but also intelligent and funny, and her friends and family had accepted me fully. We were married less than a year after she accepted my proposal, in a ceremony at the Sonoma Mission Inn in front of two hundred of our closest friends and relatives.

I had always gauged my life according to my ability to sit on an imaginary three-legged stool, the legs being my health, my financial position, and my family. At no point in my life up to the day of my wedding had I been able to sit down on that stool. That day, I did, and it felt good.

Shortly after our wedding, I commissioned our friend, the artist Mark Stock, to paint Wynne in his usual melancholy style. In it, she remains forever beautiful and untouched by the ravages to come.

# Chapter 3

# Babies on the Way

*Loneliness and lack of communication
make everything worse for everyone involved.*

EVERYTHING ABOUT WYNNE announced perfection. She was always thoughtful of those around her—more than she was of herself. Each event or evening out with her was impeccably thought through ahead of time, and her taste in clothes and style in the home were second to none. Everything was always in its place, and seemingly part of a grand plan.

After our honeymoon, Wynne and I began to "nest" immediately as we settled into our new lives together. We both wanted kids—they were part of the plan. We didn't get married solely to have children, but we definitely wanted them. We lived in a two-bedroom apartment in the heart of San Francisco on Franklin Street, and we knew that we could easily turn the guest bedroom into a nursery. It was exciting to plan and imagine how our lives would change once we had our own gaggle of kids.

Wynne was pregnant by the end of the first year of our marriage. We discovered she was pregnant by taking a home pregnancy test from the drugstore, about three weeks into January 1996. We couldn't have been more elated.

Morning sickness was definitely part of the drill, but Wynne was stoic about it, knowing that with each day, we were closer to having our first child. She was hesitant to tell anyone about the pregnancy, though, even as we entered the end of the first trimester. She was very nervous that something might go wrong.

There was reason for concern. She experienced frequent and intense aches and pains on most days.

I hated seeing her suffer. Each time we visited the doctor's office, we were on pins and needles, wondering if everything was normal or if we should be worried. Neither of us knew quite what to expect, a feeling that is probably shared by all new parents. As April approached, we could see the beginnings of life on the ultrasound, and we felt hopeful.

It was our second ultrasound visit just a few weeks later that made us fearful. The doctor told us that the placenta had started to detach a little bit from the inside of the uterine wall. Placental abruption is a serious condition. It can cause stomach pain and bleeding, which explained Wynne's symptoms. The doctor said that Wynne needed to stay off her feet as much as possible, to see if the abruption might repair itself or at least stop the tearing. We had made plans to accompany Wynne's family to Boston the following weekend to watch her father run in the Boston Marathon, but that was no longer an option. The baby was in week twenty-two of its forty-week development.

We both knew something was really wrong when blood started streaming down Wynne's leg as we sat having lunch a few days later. We rushed to the hospital, only to find out that she had miscarried. As if that wasn't horrible enough, we learned that she needed to undergo what is called a dilation and curettage (D&C) procedure to remove the dead fetus because it had matured to a size that required it. They were unable to schedule the procedure, however, until Thursday— a full five days later! Wynne was going to carry the remains of our unborn child in her uterus for five days! I was furious, and she was devastated. She couldn't stop crying. This was the worst thing either of us had ever experienced, by a long shot. We left the hospital to go home and wait.

Wynne went to lay down in bed and sleep. I couldn't keep still so I went for a run to clear my head. I felt much better after getting out, and wanted to see if I could cheer her up somehow. When I went in to check on her, though, I couldn't wake her up. I walked around to the other side of the bed, and accidentally kicked a small vodka bottle that had been emptied and then placed on the floor beside the bed. I was struck by a range of emotions at that moment: I felt overwhelmed with sadness for our tragic loss, coupled with complete horror at the discovery that my wife had the capacity to drink herself to sleep, to literally drown her sorrow.

I immediately began to rationalize the situation to ease my fear. The grief she was experiencing was compounded by the torture of carrying the dead baby inside her body for the next five days . . . maybe drinking to the point of passing out was a completely understandable response. I wasn't sure. After all, I had never experienced such an incredible loss, either. People grieve differently. All I could do was accept Wynne's feelings and try to help her get through the next five days.

After the miscarriage, it took time to adjust to our new reality. After a few weeks, I felt we needed to get our minds off the incident so we took a drive down the coast to Los Angeles, where I had grown up, to spend some time with my family and friends. This getaway served its intended purpose, for the most part, but Wynne still didn't seem like herself for a long time. Who could blame her, really? I wrestled with the knowledge that she needed to work through her emotions; that was hard for me to accept. As her husband, I felt a responsibility to try to "fix" the problem, so I put together that trip as an attempt to distract her. How else was I going to feel like I was doing something to help? It wasn't until many years later that I learned that perhaps all she needed was space, and someone to listen. Grief is a normal process but it doesn't come with a timeline.

A year later, on June 25, 1997, our first son, Preston, was born. We were nervous the entire time Wynne was pregnant, but this time everything worked out incredibly well. We were overjoyed. We'd moved out of our little two-bedroom apartment by then. Living there brought back too many bad memories for both of us. I found a spacious three-bedroom place near the center of town on California St. and Fillmore. The neighborhood was perfect—we could walk to most places and we had a great sense of community. We were even able to hire a wonderful woman, Maura, to help care for Preston and help Wynne with the housework. Having Maura would help to keep the pressure off Wynne. She was a godsend for our family over the next several years as our family grew and we found ourselves trying to care for three children under the age of five.

Harry was born sixteen months later, on October 28, 1998. It was then that we decided to begin looking at buying our first house. The only problem was that in order to afford a place big enough for our growing family, we were going to need to look outside the city... far outside the city. After discussing our financial situation with Wynne's father, we decided that the picturesque town of Danville was the best and most affordable option. I thought this was a great decision because Danville was close to Orinda where Wynne had grown up, and we already had a few friends living nearby that we could rely on initially. We found an amazing house that needed a little bit of work, but had a lot of potential.

Wynne's cousin, Denny, was a terrific help in fixing up the inside of the house. We moved into the house at the end of 1999, and our daughter, Britt, was born a few months later, on February 25, 2000. I was even able to find an apartment just a few miles away for Maura and her two children, so that Maura could continue to help out with the kids. I felt a tremendous sense of responsibility not only to my own family, but to hers as well, having shifted her children to a completely different school district and a more suburban way of life.

When I was young, my family moved five times before I was nine years old. We started out in Ohio, and then relocated to Atlanta, Milwaukee, and Chicago before finally landing in Pasadena, California. I was used to moving, but this was the first time I had created something for my family and myself. I discovered I had a passion for working out in the yard, and doing home improvement projects. This was the first time I had a chance to take pride in building something for my kids, and for us. I cleared an area in the back and put in a large wooden play structure, complete with swings, ladders, and a tree house. Behind that I put in a sport court with a backboard for hitting tennis balls, and a basketball hoop. To the right I had a semi-circular area cut into the side of the steep hill. There, I poured cement to make an outdoor grill area, complete with picnic table and serving area. Still farther past that, I cleared a large—40 x 10 foot—vegetable garden where the kids and I planted strawberries, tomatoes, beans, lettuce, and several other types of plants.

For Wynne, each pregnancy was harder than the previous one, but she was determined to build our family quickly because she didn't want to worry about her age having an adverse effect. She was, in fact, bedridden for the final six weeks before she gave birth to Britt. I remember pleading with her to agree that once Britt was born, we would stop trying to get pregnant. There was no way we were going to put her body through that again. But the argument was moot. By the time we were two months into having three kids at home, a fourth wasn't even in question. Wynne had begun her rapid decline.

# Chapter 4

# The Holiday that Wasn't

*Guilt and shame are the roots of addiction.*

LITTLE BRITT WAS just ten months old when Christmas 2000 arrived. It was our first Christmas together with all three of our children. It's still a blur to me in many ways. Wynne had been on a downward course most of the year until she was now in bed for weeks at a time, passed out from a combination of pills and alcohol. Wynne's parents, one of her brothers and his wife, and I had discussed doing an intervention while everyone was in town over the holidays. There were problems with this approach, of course. For one thing, Wynne's behavior was too unpredictable to plan for such an event. She often wasn't even conscious for the time it would take.

Three days before Christmas, I piled the kids into their car seats and got Wynne to get dressed for lunch with her parents. Our intent was to find out, ahead of the holidays and before everyone else arrived in town, if Wynne was going to be able to handle the pressure of such a large family gathering. In Wynne's family, Christmas holidays usually brought several days in a row of large social gatherings, with up to fifty people at a time from different parts of the extended family. If you were in a good state of mind, which Wynne had always seemed to be in the past, it was an incredible joyous time of year. If, on the other hand, you were having trouble, as Wynne seemed to be having now, it could be a complete nightmare.

The drive to Orinda from Danville, where we lived, has a stretch of freeway approximately thirteen miles long. Normally this would be a quick drive, but that day,

Wynne decided I was leading her into a trap. It's possible she had overheard one of my conversations with her family when we were discussing the intervention. We'd gone ahead and made plans, but the intervention was not scheduled for that day. Of course, Wynne didn't know that. She began to scream, and yelled for me to pull over so she could get out of the car. This was impossible while we were speeding down the freeway at 65 miles per hour. I was locked into a strange battle, trying to keep her from opening the front passenger door to jump out of the car, while trying to calm the kids down who were screaming in the back seat for their mommy to stop opening the door. I didn't know how to handle the situation. Should I stop and let her out at the next exit? Or should I keep going and get help from her family once we get to their house? I kept my hand pressed down tightly on the door locks and kept going, with the kids still wailing loudly. Seeing no cars at her parents' house when we pulled up, Wynne calmed down, and went inside.

"Are you planning an intervention?!" she demanded, furious. "I will *not* participate in anything like that!" We all caved, and agreed to drop the idea for now and just see how things went over the next few weeks. Maybe seeing all her relatives would be good for her, we hoped. Maybe being isolated in Danville was the reason for her behavior. I just wanted it to stop, and I was willing to consider any option.

---

The next three days were the same, though.

I sat beside our beautifully lit tree as I watched the clock on the mantel strike midnight. It was Christmas Eve 2000. We'd missed Christmas Eve dinner with Wynne's favorite cousins and their kids, who idolized and adored their Auntie Wynne. Now I was by myself in the silent living room, tears filling my eyes as I poured over directions, trying to assemble the various gifts for the kids that they would find under the tree in a few hours. I felt incredibly alone and scared. The woman I had fallen in love with not seven years before was falling apart, and I had no idea what to do about it.

"Wynne . . . Wynne," I whispered as I gently tapped her side to wake her up. "Wynne . . . time to get up, and watch the kids open presents."

"What?" She was groggy, and disoriented. "What are you talking about?"

"It's Christmas morning," I told her.

She started crying. I felt horrible for her as I tried to help her get out of bed and into the shower.

"Can we please get some help?" I pleaded.

She began sobbing uncontrollably. Before she could say a word, I handed her a piece of paper with the phone number of the Betty Ford Center.

"Let's call them, please," I implored. "I can have us there in no time."

I had packed her bag in anticipation of her positive response. After all, Christmas had always been her favorite time of the year, and I figured now was my best shot at making her realize what she was losing.

She agreed and for the first time in months, I felt a sudden surge of hope. Everything about my life had changed. There was no structure anymore. Everything was a fire drill. To make matters worse, my office was now an hour away. I remember thinking as I drove past cow pastures in the East Bay on the way to work that it would be so nice to trade places with any one of the herd. They looked so peaceful and unaware.

Britt was our third child, but Wynne's fourth pregnancy and fourth delivery by surgery—one D&C and three cesarean sections in just five years. In the months that followed Britt's birth in February, Wynne's mood changed dramatically. She began to stay in bed longer each day, allowing Maura to take on increasingly more responsibility for daily life with the kids. She kept complaining that she still had pain—and who was I to second-guess her after I had witnessed the amount of pain she went through *during* the pregnancies themselves. Even though the C-sections had all been performed at the California Pacific Medical Center in San Francisco, we now lived in Danville, so Wynne had developed relationships with a new set of local doctors, both medical and psychiatric.

At the time, I believed we were doing the right thing by combining the expertise of the two groups of medical professionals in our quest to find relief from the mental and physical pain she was experiencing, but looking back, this may have unwittingly given her the opportunity to begin what later became a "doctor shopping spree." None of the doctors were communicating with one another, and I wasn't savvy enough to think about the potential consequences of that.

After all, these were professionals, trained to take care of their patients, not to over-medicate them. I simply assumed that Wynne was following a protocol designed for the optimal outcome over time. I believed that the pain she was experiencing was something that I simply could not comprehend, so I went along with the recommended treatments and put my faith in Wynne's ability to make the right choices.

As we approached the fifth month since her last pregnancy, things were getting worse instead of better. I began to question the doctors she was visiting. Why did she have so many prescriptions? Why so many different medications over the past few months? Why was she taking opiates and benzodiazepines—and other drugs as well—in combination? Why did she still have pain? I could understand continuing to experience emotional pain, given what I had been reading about postpartum depression, but surely the physical pain should have subsided by now?

I didn't realize it then, but Wynne really was trying to find a way to withdraw from her newfound addiction in the early stages of this ordeal. I remember seeing several bottles of Suboxone around the house. Suboxone is sometimes used for chronic pain relief, but I now know that it is also prescribed to treat opiate addiction and withdrawal. However, it only works if it is used properly, and if it is just one component of a comprehensive plan. I wish I had been part of the discussions with Wynne's doctors, because maybe together we could have nipped her growing drug dependence in the bud. Studies have shown that the longer a substance use disorder (SUD) goes unaddressed, the harder it is to treat, because for all intents and purposes, your brain is being rewired.

Wynne was unable to talk to me about her drug use, and later addiction, even in the early stages. In this regard, Wynne and I were not unique; the same thing happens in so many families. Shame prevents those with the substance issue from reaching out. In Wynne's case, I also believe she felt capable of beating it on her own.

As the months wore on, however, she had convinced the doctors that she had severe anxiety, and therefore needed the benzodiazepine—benzos—to be able to take care of the kids, to get through the day, to function. In fact, however, it was the benzos that were turning her into the zombie she had become. What's worse, Maura and I had enabled Wynne to sink into this zombie state by taking over her responsibilities. We were not allowing her to face the consequences of her actions. But at the time, that didn't seem like a viable option. We had three kids in diapers—they needed care, no matter what state their mother was in.

There were so many pill containers around the house. They came in all sizes and shapes, with labels in various colors. I really had no idea what she was taking. I had allowed her to continue ramping the prescriptions she was getting, and now the situation had taken on a life of its own. She wasn't communicating with me about what was going on, and had stopped allowing me to come to her appointments.

I now know that the benzos were Wynne's self-prescribed temporary antidote during times when she was detoxing from opiates because she was unable to find a doctor or pharmacy to fill another prescription. When she couldn't obtain benzos either, she would turn to alcohol. Anything to stop the shakes and the pain of withdrawal.

I picked up the phone to call the Betty Ford Center.

"Merry Christmas! This is the Betty Ford Center. How may I help you?"

"Hi. I'd like to find out if you have room for my wife today?" I asked hopefully.

"Oh . . . I'm sorry. We don't admit patients today, unfortunately. We could take her tomorrow morning, though." She sounded sincere.

"Please. *Please.* Can you make an exception today? I'm not sure we can make it tomorrow. She agreed to seek help for the first time today, and I don't know what tomorrow will be like." I was desperate.

"I'm sorry, sir. We can make a reservation for tomorrow, though. That's all I can do." I reluctantly made the reservation, hoping it would be okay.

I hung up feeling completely defeated. I had no idea what the rest of the day, much less tomorrow, would bring.

It was Christmas Day. We were supposed to go to her parents' house in a few hours to celebrate the holiday. It had seemed like a good idea back when we made the plans, but now, looking at Wynne's swollen face and red eyes, it seemed impossible. How were we going to do that?!

I had figured that if I could just get her to her parents' house, where her own family and her cousins, nieces, and nephews would be gathering to open presents and share a meal, maybe she would remember how much she loved the holidays, and feel motivated to stop the spiral. After all, Christmas was always her favorite time of year. As the youngest in her family, she saw her role as the person who brought everyone back together around the holidays. She was the one who maintained the family traditions. She was the planner, the glue that kept the extended family together. She was happy to orchestrate most of the events surrounding Christmas at her parents' house in order to make sure her siblings and close family felt special and loved. Her favorite holiday tradition was taking her nieces—who ranged in age from five to ten years old when I first met them—out together for a night on the town in a limousine, and then bringing them home for scary movies and popcorn. To them, she was Aunt Wynne—the fun aunt, the favorite.

Looking back, she did in fact react the way I thought she would, at least at first. She got ready and we all headed over to her parents' house. Wynne tried to participate in the festivities as best she could, but she wasn't herself. She wasn't fully present for the holiday she had always looked forward to more than anything, and I believe the guilt and shame she felt might have driven her to escape into drugs and alcohol that day, even though we were in public. I tried hard to conceal my feelings of fear and shock when I glanced at her, but I've never been really good at hiding what I'm thinking. Her eyes flickered back and forth between hating herself for acting the way she was, and hating me for allowing it. If she would just stop, and get back to being the person I knew was still in there somewhere, we'd be okay. But that didn't happen. By midday she was a wreck, and her mother told her to go sleep in her bedroom. Wynne shut the door and we didn't see her the rest of the day.

The next morning, I loaded her suitcase in the car, and dropped the kids off at her parents' house. I could see Wynne's expression turning into one of dread and anger as we drove away from our kids.

"Turn around!" she screamed. "I can't do this! The kids can't be without me for a whole month. I won't do it!"

I kept driving, but this was what I had feared most. As her mind started to clear, she was coming to understand what was actually happening, and it wasn't a pleasant realization. What would her family and friends think? Shame. All she could say was, "I can't leave my kids." All I was thinking was, "You already have! How could it get worse?"

Well, needless to say, it did.

# Chapter 5

# Seeking Help

*The key to letting go of guilt and shame is self-acceptance.*
*But that doesn't come easy. The hardest person to forgive is yourself.*

"I WILL NOT STAND here in back of a bunch of niggers and spics!"

My mouth dropped open in shock at her words.

The Oakland Airport was a complete disaster even at 7:00 a.m. It was the day after Christmas, and Wynne had agreed to let me take her to the resort town of Palm Springs; from there we would rent a car and drive to the Betty Ford Center, which in reality felt more like a last resort. The lines were so long at the airport that I was convinced we would miss our flight. I couldn't let that happen, so I was frantically trying to bribe a porter to take our bags and check us in so that I could keep Wynne from leaving the airport to go back home. She was flaming pissed that she was leaving the kids, and maybe withdrawing a bit as well.

Lately, she had become increasingly verbally abusive to people in public settings. A few weeks earlier, she had even called a four-year-old classmate of Preston's a "little whore" when the girl lifted her dress to chew on it while the class was singing Christmas carols at their preschool Christmas pageant. The parents around us were staring fiercely and whispering as Wynne dared them to say something back. I had to quickly remove her from the auditorium and wait outside for Preston to be finished. I was sharing my life with this woman and I didn't know who she was anymore. I would later come to understand that opiates change a person's personality. Anger and aggression are often on display when people are coming down from a high. They have a short fuse. Eventually they become unrecognizable from the person they used to be before drugs. This was *not* the woman I knew. This was definitely not Wynne.

No one would take our bags and check us in, and as the situation became more dangerous with the crowd clearly not appreciating Wynne's use of epithets, I decided to grab her and run for the car. Within minutes, I was driving to Palm Springs at speeds of 90 to 100 mph. We were both angry, but for different reasons. She was furious with me because I was taking her away from her home and her kids, and I'm sure she felt shame that her family knew where she was going and why she was going there. I was angry because I had married a woman I thought I knew, but now felt no connection with. The woman sitting in the passenger seat beside me was abusive and unpredictable. She was a stranger.

We hadn't made it more than fifty miles down the highway before Wynne asked me to stop at a gas station so she could use the restroom. At least we were far enough out of town that I was confident we would continue on to Southern California. We were too far away from our house for her to easily make her way back home. I stopped at the Chevron station off of Interstate 5 near Patterson and she leaped out of the car and ran into the store. While I waited for her to return, I filled up the gas tank. Soon she emerged from the store with a twelve-pack of beer in hand. I knew she had already taken a handful of Valium during the drive, which I had no problem with as I hoped it would put her to sleep. This was a different story. We argued for several minutes before I conceded, and let her get in the car with the beer. I had absolutely no leverage, and on some level, I actually wanted her to pass out so I wouldn't have to listen to her berate me anymore.

She drank herself to sleep over the next hour, and I continued on to Palm Springs. I envisioned the Betty Ford Center as the finish line that I desperately needed to cross before my wife woke up again. They would surely be able to help her understand what she was doing to herself, and we could get back to being the family we were meant to be.

As I drove into the entrance to the clinic, I felt a profound sense of relief. I had actually made it. My hands were frozen in place from the stress of gripping the wheel; I had just driven nearly five hundred miles in less than seven hours. As I pulled up in front, Wynne woke up, as she had done so many times, in a complete fog, not knowing where she was or what she was doing there. The admissions director helped us with her bags as we walked slowly into the facility. I think Wynne actually had a bit of hope at that moment as well because she didn't argue or fight. It was the first time I saw her actually frightened, and sad as she fully understood where she was now. My heart sank, and I hugged her, and made sure she knew I would be there for her when she was ready to come home. I meant it, too. It was moments like these over the years to come that kept me involved and gave me hope.

She lasted three days.

"Mr. Doyle? Mrs. Doyle has checked out."

"What? Where did she go?" I said in complete disbelief.

"She didn't say, but she's standing at the driveway entrance. She appears to be trying to wave down a cab." They had obviously seen this happen before, and they knew that the only ones who begin to recover are the ones who *want* to be there.

Wynne didn't have a cell phone, and in any case I knew there was no way she was going to call me. I didn't know what to do so I waited to see if she would catch a flight home. A few hours passed, and no one heard from her. I began calling the various airlines, but no one would confirm if she was on a flight or not.

More time passed, and nothing. I called our credit card companies to see if she'd made any purchases from anywhere, and nothing. It was excruciating. Earlier, we had gone ahead and hired a woman who was going to lead us in an intervention over the holidays, but when Wynne agreed to go to the Betty Ford facility, I'd cancelled. Now I called her back, and asked what to do. Within a few minutes she and I had a plan to find Wynne and bring her home.

We couldn't leave until the following morning, but with the interventionist at my side, I found myself driving to Palm Springs for the second time in four days. This time, however, the time I spent that day on the road is a complete blur. Shaking with anxiety, all I could do was curse the highway signs that told me I was still several hours away. My mind kept playing morbid scenarios over and over. How would I find her, and when I did, what kind of shape would she be in?

I drove around the city of Rancho Mirage, feeling helpless. At least I was *there*, though. Now I was close enough to do something—that is, if I could find her.

I made more phone calls to a few of our credit card companies.

*Yes!* She had finally used one of the credit cards.

─────

The clerk at the front desk told us which room was hers, and we headed up the stairs. Without stopping to knock, I twisted the handle and the door swung open, but I couldn't see anything. The lights were off and the curtains were drawn. It smelled like a homeless encampment. Was she really here?

There were two beds in the room; one of the mattresses had been turned over and lay diagonal to the box spring. I couldn't hold my feelings in check anymore. I was completely overwhelmed. This was worse than I had even imagined during my drive.

Unable to see anything through the tears, I continued to look for her. On the table was a nearly empty gallon bottle of Ketel One vodka and two large bottles of NyQuil, also nearly empty.

I found her lying beneath a blanket sprawled on the floor at the far side of the room. She had not been able to make it to the bathroom, apparently. She was unconscious.

"Let's get her cleaned up and into the back of the car," the intervention specialist sighed.

She had seen it many times. I, on the other hand, was in shock. My ears were ringing. I felt like I was floating.

"Shouldn't we get her to a hospital?" I wondered aloud. The intervention specialist obviously had a plan, though, and I was just going to have to follow it.

Wynne woke up briefly on the drive, and then fell back asleep. The NyQuil she had taken was obviously keeping her down, which in a way was a blessing.

"Turn right up ahead, and drive about a mile up the hill," instructed the intervention specialist, guiding me.

We had driven a little over two hours to reach Creative Care in Malibu. Before Christmas, the intervention specialist and I had discussed this facility during planning meetings for the intervention. If we'd gone through with our plans and held it, one desired outcome was for Wynne to come here and try to get to the root of her issues. Creative Care is known as a "dual diagnosis" facility, because it treats not only substance abuse, but also mental health. During the meetings, I'd learned that in many cases, the two are intertwined. At this point, I was willing to try just about anything.

The intervention specialist and I had barely spoken during the drive; both of us were focused on getting Wynne to our destination before she woke up. Who knew how she'd react?

As we pulled up to the front of the facility, we were greeted by a team of medical personnel.

"What has she been taking, and how much?" There was a definite sense of urgency as they pulled her out of the back of the car and took her inside.

They explained the detoxification process to me, and the appropriate time frame needed for each stage of recovery. I realized my hands were still clenched, and I ached all over. It felt like I had been in a car crash. These days, the tension was constant, but finding Wynne in that situation brought it in waves so powerful that my heart felt like it was going to come out of my chest. I had become used to the stress, but this was beyond anything I could have imagined a year earlier.

Little did I know it was only going to get worse.

# Chapter 6

# Relapse

*You can't fix people... especially if they don't want to be fixed.*

THE NEXT FEW weeks passed quickly as the kids and I were able to step back and catch our breath without the constant angry chaos in the house. Each weekend, we would pile into our SUV, which I had pre-loaded with new toys and games to keep them busy, and head off to see mommy.

The kids were too young to understand much of anything that was going on, so it was fairly easy to make it fun for them. I pretended we were going on an adventure. When we arrived the first time in Malibu, I could tell Wynne was totally overwhelmed and grateful to see us. She told the kids that it was a cooking school, and that she was there to learn to be a better cook so that she could make special meals at home for us. This was a white lie that would perpetuate itself until the kids were old enough to absorb the real story. It wasn't until Little Britt was eight years old that she told me how crushed she had felt back then by her perception that her mother was making a conscious choice to leave her for something she thought was more important than spending time with the kids. I discovered at that moment that there is an excruciatingly fine line between protecting your children from the truth, and helping them understand the truth at their level of understanding. When the kids were older and we could discuss what was really happening, I would tell them that it wasn't their fault, it had nothing to do with them, but even I thought it had something to do with me, and I was the adult.

The specialists at the facility held discussions with Wynne and me to help repair the damage, and to help me understand the protocol she was working through. It all seemed logical based on the withdrawals I had seen her live through. She already looked a hundred times better after the first week. I had all kinds of hope that hadn't existed for months. I think we both thought this was going to work.

---

February 2001 started out really well. Wynne was home. She'd completed her detox program. Now she was trying very hard to make up for lost time with the kids, and she and I were getting along. We started having people over again, and even worked together on the vegetable garden outside with the kids. I wanted to believe so badly that it had all been a really bad dream that I trusted she was "cured." What I didn't realize, though, was that her cravings for opiates had never gone away, and her contacts who had prescribed them before were all too willing to continue supplying. It was happening right under my nose. What I didn't realize at the time was that pharmaceutical companies were really picking up their incentive programs for doctors to prescribe their poison.

I met a woman a few years ago who had been a drug representative for one of the companies making opioids between 2000 and 2002. Her job was to boost sales of these lucrative drugs, and to that end, she offered all kinds of perks. She described to me how she would invite doctors to attend a seminar, and as a thank-you for their time, she would send them and their families skiing for a week. Of course, not all of the gifts were that lavish. She would walk through a medical complex, and invite everyone to fill up their tanks at the gas station around the corner while she discussed the merits of opiates with them. Free food, free drinks, and offers of consulting and speaking fees were dangled like bait. Her conscience got the better of her, and she quit her job after two years, but she remembers to this day how slimy she felt promoting the beginnings of the epidemic we live with today.

Things began to deteriorate when I found a prescription bottle that had recently been filled. Wynne had only been back from detox for four or five weeks. Not only did I feel betrayed and lied to, I felt violated that some doctor had reached into my life again, and spread disease where I thought it was gone. Wynne and I fought as she denied everything. That made me angrier. At one point, my daughter, who was barely a year old and still learning to walk, found a pill and swallowed it. The pill bottle was hidden under the counter in our bathroom, and was half full of Valium. The only way I knew what she had taken was that she lay there on the floor staring limply up at me with the bottle in her hand. I called 911 immediately, and Wynne and I sat with her for what seemed to be an eternity until the paramedics got there. The incident was treated as an accident, so there were no legal repercussions concerning charges of poor parenting. Still, I was white hot with rage. No more fucking pills in my house! Of course, Wynne agreed. We were both shaken to the core.

It was only four or five weeks before I found a new pill bottle. This one had a local doctor's name on it that I didn't recognize.

I think the combination of my angry reaction and Wynne's feelings of guilt over Little Britt's incident with the pill stepped up her downward spiral, which quickly went out of control. She was now drinking heavily and taking pills in different combinations just to numb the pain. Before the holidays, she'd suggested that maybe her suburban isolation from our friends in San Francisco might be one of the causes, as well. I wish I could say that I remember discussing that with her, but I don't. The only thing I knew was that Danville wasn't working for us. Less than a month after Little Britt swallowed that pill, I put the house on the market and began looking for a broker in San Francisco who would be able to help us find something with at least a little bit of yard. I was very sad to see the work I had put into the kids' play area and the garden in the last eighteen months go to waste, but I needed to make some choices. Maybe this would help Wynne snap out of it.

Little did I know that listing the house would bring a whole new set of issues into play, as Wynne was completely unable to function with prospective buyers walking through the house at showings. One morning that summer, Maura called in sick and Wynne didn't wake up. I wouldn't have even known if not for a real estate agent who came knocking on the door. Preston answered it in his pajamas at 9:00 a.m. Back then, I left for work at 4:30 a.m. on those days I made the sixty-mile trek each way between Danville and Menlo Park, so it was typically several hours into my day before I would normally hear from anyone at home. I was also very focused on work at that period in my life, because my wealth management practice had begun to do really well. I'm fairly certain that Preston could feel the anxiety creeping in to his life at that point—at age five. The real estate agent stayed there with the kids while I raced home, cursing the other motorists in my way. If the frantic fifty-five-minute drive back to the house didn't generate high enough levels of anxiety for me, the disgusted looks on the faces of the real estate agent and her clients were enough to make me want to crawl into a hole. That was the first time I worried about Child Protective Services paying us a visit. It was also the first time Wynne was taken away in an ambulance with a blood alcohol level over .4.

I was still working three days a week in Menlo Park while Maura helped make sure the house ran smoothly. Wynne kept hitting new lows, passing out for days at a time, each time with a different excuse. At one point she tried to convince me she had been bitten by a brown recluse, a type of venomous spider that was in the news at the time for supposedly having spread to California, far from its native habitat. Those rumors eventually were proven to be false, but that day Wynne persuaded me that she desperately needed to go to the hospital. We went, but as I suspected, she was simply looking to get a new opiate prescription filled. You might be thinking at this point that I had the power to make sure doctors knew what she was doing, and to stop them from giving her the prescriptions, but everything I said fell on deaf ears, and that's when they were listening. Doctors and pharmacists had no obligation to me, and in fact, told me many times that they could not discuss my wife's medical situation with me unless she consented.

That never happened.

# Chapter 7

# The Big Picture

*Prescription drug overdose is an epidemic in the United States.*
*All too often, and in far too many communities,*
*the treatment is becoming the problem.*

—CDC Director Thomas Frieden

THE CONSEQUENCES OF prescription pain relievers are devastating and on the rise. The number of unintentional overdose deaths from prescription pain pills has more than quadrupled since 1999. According to the Center for Disease Control (CDC), every day in the United States, forty-six people die as a result of opioid drug overdose, and another thousand are treated in emergency departments for the misuse or abuse of these same drugs. In my home state, California, there were 4,395 deaths attributed to opioid overdose in 2014 alone. That's one death every forty-five minutes. According to the Partnership for Drug Free Kids, more than 17 percent of California's health care costs are related to opioid abuse, the highest percentage in the country. California isn't alone, however. The prescription drug epidemic has hit every state and every demographic. Drugs now kill more Americans than cars, and many states have more yearly opioid prescriptions than people. America's growing abuse of opioids took place under the radar for several years until it burst into the news as a full-blown crisis.

We used to associate drug overdoses with the homeless person lurking in the shadows buying heroin or meth from a street dealer. That street dealer now wears a white lab coat and dispenses the drugs legally through a respectable pharmacy system to which anyone has access; that buyer is the soccer mom, the student athlete, and the construction worker trying to keep his job. Because the drugs come in pill form and are prescribed by a doctor, their use is almost socially acceptable. Many, like me, had no idea that our medicine cabinets could be so dangerous; OxyContin, Vicodin, and Percocet are among the worst offenders. In many cases, those who need to get the high more quickly are actually grinding the pills into powder and snorting it.

The typical scenario seems to be that someone has an injury of some kind, or perhaps undergoes a routine surgery, and is prescribed painkillers during their recuperation period to help them get through the day. In our case, my wife had a particularly difficult cesarean delivery for the birth of her third child, and she was prescribed Vicodin for the resulting pain so that she would be able to get up out of bed and take care of the baby. Neither of us was warned about the extreme danger of prolonged use. Some of us are more prone to addiction, without question, but I'd wager that most of those who are prone to the disease would not knowingly seek out a substance that would ultimately ruin their lives and the lives of those around them. That is the ultimate outrage in this situation. We place our trust in our doctors, particularly given their Hippocratic Oath to "do no harm."

In many cases, student athletes, competing for spots on the team or scholarships to college, get injured, and are prescribed opioids to enable them to "play through the pain" while they heal. After several weeks of recovery, they find they are addicted to the pain medication. Too embarrassed to tell their parents, they turn to heroin because they either can't get another prescription or they can't afford to pay for it, and the withdrawal symptoms are too much to bear. Heroin gives the same sense of euphoria at a fraction of the price. From there, the story is seen across the country in newspapers every day.

The scariest addition to this crisis is the street use of the drug fentanyl, a powerful and quick-acting synthetic opioid. Although the drug has been around, like most opioids, since the 1960s, its popularity climbed over the past several decades and by 2012, it was the most widely used synthetic opioid on the market. Through my work this past year on the Alcohol and Other Drug (AOD) Advisory Board to the Marin County Board of Supervisors, I learned that drug dealers have invested in pill presses so that they can crush prescription opioid pills, and add the drug fentanyl to the mix before "re-forming" the pill to sell on the street. Fentanyl is fifty to one hundred times more potent than morphine and can kill instantly if it is administered improperly.

The naked eye cannot tell the difference between a safe dose and a lethal dose when compared side by side.

Overdoses can occur with the smallest amount, and buyers are unaware how much fentanyl has been added into the drugs they purchase on the street.

One group, Shatterproof, is making a difference, however, through creating community and by changing laws that cover prescriptions. Two years ago, I reached out to Gary Mendell, founder of Shatterproof, after searching the web for groups I could join to discuss how to stop the epidemic. Gary and his group are an inspiration for those working through drug abuse issues in their family, and the work they are doing to help change the way we address the problem is revolutionary.

I never understood the advice I sometimes heard to let Wynne hit rock bottom. I knew that criticizing her only made her feel worse about the things she was doing. Sometimes, though, I was so angry with her and with the situation I found us in that I couldn't help myself. Shatterproof believes that shame and stigma perpetuate the disease, and I agree. Coming out of the shadows, admitting the problem, and discussing addiction openly not only helps the person afflicted with the disease, but also the family working through the devastating series of events. Feeling alone in this battle is the absolute worst part.

# Chapter 8

# A Change of Scenery to Break the Cycle

*We can run from our inner problems for a while, but we shouldn't be too surprised when external solutions don't truly solve them.*

WE HAD BEEN LOOKING at one particular house in San Francisco, but the price was just a bit too high, and the place needed work. I wasn't afraid of the work because I—once again wrongly—thought that a project was just what Wynne needed; it would get her focused on something that she would feel good about.

A few months passed and we were still house hunting. Then the 9/11 terror attacks occurred. In the unsettled aftermath of those terrible events, fear in the financial and real estate markets allowed us to purchase the house we wanted at a lower price. I thought this would be the answer, for sure. After all, Wynne had told me point-blank that she was lonely, and that if we moved back to San Francisco, she would be fine again. I thought the root of the issue was isolation.

The house had been empty for several months, because the elderly woman who owned it had passed away. There was, however, a family of raccoons living there. They had taken up residence in the space between the ceiling of the first floor and the floorboards of the second floor.

We moved into a short-term rental apartment just down the street while the necessary work took place on the house. Maura and her kids moved back to San Francisco with us, and they now lived in a separate part of the rental apartment while Maura got her feet on the ground and figured out how to make everything work for her family. I felt guilty about uprooting her again so soon after having moved her and her kids to the East Bay only a few years earlier, so this time, when we finally moved into the new house a few months later, I made sure to help her with a down payment on a place of her own.

The first day of demolition in the downstairs part of the house was exciting. It was the beginning of 2002, and Wynne seemed hopeful. The kids were running around the outside of the house trying to look inside, but the windows were covered.

Wynne and I were as curious as the kids were at this point so I opened the door and we all walked in. I could see from the look on the kids' faces that they didn't know what to think. I looked at them with pretend anger on my face, and said sternly, "I don't know who did this, but I'm going to find them, and make them fix it!" Then I burst out laughing at their shocked expressions. It was a moment of levity that brought everything into perspective for me. Houses are one thing; people are another.

Although my intention had been to give Wynne a project to focus on, she was completely unable to function on a daily basis, and so I again picked up the slack, making the barrage of decisions that needed to be made in order for the work on the house to be completed on time. I believe this was just one more in a series of things that she would "fail" at, plunging her deeper into guilt and self-hatred.

A few months into the project, I came home to find Wynne walking out of the house in her pajamas. I asked her where she going, and got no response—only a look that told me to mind my own business. This was normal in those days, as she was now within walking distance of drugstores and liquor stores in our new temporary neighborhood.

This time, I wanted to see where she went. I wanted to see just who would possibly sell liquor to an obviously intoxicated and overmedicated woman. She had no idea I was following thirty feet behind her as she walked three blocks to the small local grocery store near us. I had been there a few times myself for small things I had forgotten to get at Safeway, but as I walked in, I could tell right away that Wynne had clearly established a very friendly rapport with the man behind the checkout counter. She still hadn't noticed that I was there, as I walked in only seconds behind her and hid in the next aisle over. She was both deliberate and unapologetic as she purchased a large bottle of vodka.

After she left the store, I stayed behind to talk to the man behind the counter. I wanted to demand of him how he could in good conscience sell that bottle of liquor to a woman when he could clearly see she was already intoxicated. I wanted him to know that she had a family; she had little kids. When I confronted him, I quickly learned that he already knew all about our family. He knew about the kids, the move, the house we bought, the work we were doing on it—everything. It was apparently only I who had an issue with selling alcohol by the half gallon to someone whose state of mind was such that she floated through the store, bottle in hand, not paying any attention to the way she was dressed or how she was slurring. The man told me that he was running a business that was taking care of his family, and, as he said to me, "I'm only doing what's best for me and my family. *You* need to take care of yours." He was right, but once again, I was the one who felt alone in this battle.

The next morning, I asked Maura to watch the kids, even though it was Saturday, and went for a run to get a feel for the neighborhood. The place we were renting was only five blocks from the home we were refurbishing. I took off at a good pace, trying to lose myself in my own thoughts as I had done so many times back in high school when I ran cross country. Running had always helped me through difficult times by giving me the mental space to turn things over in my mind from several angles. What was I missing? Why couldn't I fix my life?

As I approached the corner of Taraval Street and 19th Avenue, I saw a karate school called One Martial Arts, with kids running around inside. They looked like they were having a ball. The scene had an energy that drew me in. What seemed like chaos at first glance was actually the teacher's way of keeping the kids engaged as he systematically taught them concepts like focus, respect, and gratitude. I sat down and watched for a bit until the instructor, Professor Brannon Beliso, came over to greet me. It was our first meeting, and I'm still grateful for it. Preston was definitely old enough for karate, and Harry was on the cusp, so I signed them both up that day. Little Britt would join them a few years later as one of the youngest students at just four years old. It was an incredibly rewarding endeavor for us as the kids earned not only belts through the system, but also individual badges that reinforced the hard work they were putting in. I joined as well, and soon we were there every Tuesday and Thursday after school, and on

Saturdays for family workshops. Brannon had a kick-boxing class as well, and every once in a while I was able to get Wynne to participate in that. She even dived in at full speed a few months later after another 30-day treatment stay. It was my place of grounding. I felt that perhaps this was the place that could positively impact our family, and get us back on track.

For the next few years, we skated through our lives, with me holding my breath to see if Wynne could some-how pull it together as we made new friends, and tried very hard to focus on a healthy lifestyle. I had guarded hope. I say that because I had been filled with hope so many times before, only to see her crash again. This time, though, she lasted almost two years before need-ing to be taken to the hospital again.

# Chapter 9

# If You're Not Part
# of the Solution

*Take care of yourself.*
*You can't help others if you can't help yourself.*

"OKAY, WE HAVE someone new this morning who has joined us. Would you like to share your first name, and a little bit about your story?"

It was the first time I had ever attended an Al-Anon meeting. It was now April 2004, four years since everything began to fall apart. We had relocated to San Francisco in late 2001, hoping that the move back to the city where we had first met would relieve Wynne's isolation and help her focus on getting treatment that would stick this time. I thought she would realize how much I cared by giving up the house I'd worked so hard on and moving us back to the city where her friends lived, and where we had made so many great memories during the '90s. This choice, however, was the beginning of my financial downfall. We had moved to Danville to buy our first house because we couldn't afford to buy in San Francisco yet. Now here I was, taking on massive mortgage debt in an attempt to make Wynne happy. My business was growing at a rapid pace, but not fast enough.

Today was particularly painful. Wynne woke up at 5:15 a.m., crying and asking where the kids were. She had been passed out now for several days in a row, ever since the party we had agreed to host at our house with several of our friends with children we had met at school. I had agreed to the party thinking it would give her something to concentrate on and feel good about, even though I knew that parties we had hosted in the past had ended with her in bed, high on whatever concoction would put her to sleep and keep her demons at bay. She inevitably felt miserable as she contemplated why the party that I and everyone else thought was amazing had not been "perfect." There it was again: "perfect." By this point in my marriage, I absolutely hated that word. Wynne strived so hard to live up to a standard that was clearly impossible, and the consequences were obvious.

Although the last few years had shown small sparks of the old Wynne, enough to keep me engaged and hopeful, every day was a crapshoot. By now, though, the pattern was easy to see. After working her way through another 30-day treatment program and coming out looking great and all smiles, she would either do something to hurt herself or simply feign sickness so that she could go to urgent care. She had figured out the right combination of words to describe her symptoms so that she would get Vicodin. From there, over the next few days, she would see as many doctors as she could at different facilities all around San Francisco to get more prescriptions. The Mission District was particularly appealing to her as she could visit several clinics in a small area and come away with several prescriptions. She would revisit those same clinics and care facilities ten or fifteen days later for refills. At the height of her addiction, she'd be consuming up to forty pills per day.

Once the doctors cut her off—which would often be as long as two to three months later—the withdrawals would begin. Benzodiazepines were next, and they were to help her combat "anxiety." It only takes a few of those to lift you into a zombie-like state. Sometimes it looked like she was just floating through the room, completely unaware that anyone was near. The last stage was alcohol. Once the pills ran out, likely because she couldn't function well enough under the influence of the benzos to get more, she would drink herself to sleep—for days and weeks at a time.

This cycle had repeated itself over and over during the last four years. By now, Wynne had attended five different programs, and one a second time. Each time it was the same: she would wake up one morning after months of decline, and agree that she needed to get help. Every third week or so, the rehab centers would hold a "Family Week," when I would listen to lectures, participate in workshops, share our story, and attend therapy sessions with Wynne. Sometimes I learned a few things, but I always left feeling more depressed than when I had arrived. Nothing was changing—in fact, things were getting worse, and Wynne was beginning to resent me as much as I resented her. Neither one of us was able to see beyond the incredible pain we were each experiencing in different ways.

One of the big concepts I learned about at these workshops was "enabling." It's when your actions, however well-meaning, contribute to the self-destructive behavior of the person with the substance abuse issue. I struggled every day with that definition. It wasn't because I didn't understand it. On the surface, it makes complete sense. The problem was applying it to real-life situations. Wynne was my wife and the mother of my three young children. Should I leave the kids alone in her care or should I always make certain that someone else was home with them? Should I always be the designated driver or should I let her possibly get a DUI? When was my behavior helping and supporting Wynne, and when was it only allowing the situation to continue and even worsen? I had to make decisions daily, many of which involved either my family's safety in some way, or the safety of someone outside our family if Wynne managed to get behind the wheel of a car.

Therapists would constantly remind me that addicts need to have consequences in order to make changes in their behavior. If those consequences negatively affect my kids, do I allow them to happen? If the consequences are monetary, but I'm ultimately the sole breadwinner, do I allow them to happen? And finally, if the consequences cause further guilt and shame, doesn't that seem base? My life was a massive tug of war between what Wynne needed, what the kids needed, and what I needed. Although I lost most of the time, it felt like I won enough times, and in enough ways, to get through it. In my mind, it felt like I was at one end of a large swamp, trying to slog my way to the other end every day.

Growing up, I was taught that "you finish what you start." I always took that to mean that you don't give up. I was also taught that you help those in need, and treat others with the respect you wanted to be treated with yourself. This idea of watching the mother of my children fall to rock bottom was foreign to everything I'd been raised to believe. Being an enabler shielded Wynne from the negative consequences of addiction, and that wasn't good. But was just standing by while she experienced rock bottom really the answer? How could we possibly recover from that?

Wynne was a master, too, of sensing when I was ready to give up on her. At those moments, she'd come through with a vulnerable look in her eye or a pleading whimper. She would promise to change and I believed her. I had hope.

The day I went to my first Al-Anon meeting, I stayed home from work. My friends had been encouraging me for months to find a meeting of some kind that I could attend regularly and get some support. Now seemed like a good opportunity. That morning, I took the kids to school, and then drove to a church on 19th Avenue where there was an Al-Anon meeting that allowed newcomers.

I walked in expecting a large crowd, but was greeted by a small group of about a dozen individuals who showed a combination of serenity and angst that I had not experienced anywhere else. These were people who had chosen to save themselves. They had come to the conclusion that there was nothing they could do for their loved ones if they didn't want to help themselves first. The families that I had met at Wynne's various short-term rehab programs were still in the infancy of the disease. They still had hope that they could cure their loved ones.

As I sat there listening to each person update the rest of the group about their lives, or introduce themselves for the first time, I started to feel my face turn red with anticipation that I had to talk. As I opened my mouth to say my name, nothing came out. I cleared my throat and opened and closed my mouth a few more times, but I couldn't utter a single word. I was overcome by a wave of anxiety and sadness. I hadn't ever been in a safe, caring environment where I felt the people I was with truly understood what I was going through, and I didn't know how to handle it. I had no ability whatsoever to speak for the first time in my life. The meeting ended without me getting anything out, but I vowed to return the following week to try again.

But I didn't. In fact, I never went back. I regret that decision now, but at that time, it was just too painful for me to be present.

On my way home from the meeting, I decided to stop by the karate studio and talk to Brannon Beliso, the instructor. After all, this had become my grounding place; the people and the practice had given me a family and a focus. Luckily, Brannon was in the back in his office.

I don't know what I expected, but it sure wasn't that I would sit down and burst into tears in front of a man I respected, one who was teaching my kids and me every other day. But that's exactly what I did. I couldn't help myself. We sat there for over an hour, talking honestly about what was happening to my family. Brannon was empathetic and had personal experiences to share with me. He and I discussed how to really focus on the kids to help them through everything. It was on that spur-of-the-moment visit that we forged what was to become the friendship that helped me keep centered over the next several years through martial arts training and meditation. Brannon's goal is to foster self-discipline, self-confidence, and self-respect in his students. His exhortation to "live your best life" has helped me in my quest to remain present since that day.

# Chapter 10

# Falling Apart

*You need a support network that includes professional providers, people who share a similar situation, family, friends, and members of your church or religious organization.*

LOOKING BACK AT the beginning of Wynne's addiction, I remember feeling so alone and scared. I wondered if there was something I had done to trigger it. Was it moving away from the city? Should I have shown more support over the years by giving up alcohol myself? Should I have done more research and been more involved in her medication regimen early on? I had so many questions.

After we moved back to San Francisco, we started making more friends as the kids entered grade school. There were soccer, basketball, and baseball games (multiply sports activities by three kids). There were school functions, and occasional family get-togethers. Our core group of friends began to expand, and feel like family after a while.

But things weren't so rosy. I was very busy, between commuting to Menlo Park four days a week and taking care of the family. The kids were beginning to need more of my time and energy. The activities they were involved in were also a welcome mental break from Wynne's issues. Although it sounds like we were starting to build a life with our newfound friends, the truth is that we were skating a very fine line between keeping up appearances and completely falling apart.

In public situations, Wynne was a master of disguise. If anyone suspected that she was having substance abuse issues, they were quickly convinced otherwise when they saw her out in public. I think we both wanted badly to be able to say that nothing was wrong. Everything was going so well on every other front.

It had been several months since the last treatment program, and Wynne seemed to be headed down her same path again. I decided to try something different this time—I'd heard about something that perhaps we could do together and that might actually work. Sanoviv Medical Institute in Baja, Mexico, focused on healing the whole person through the concept of functional medicine. Their practitioners dive into their patients' histories, looking at the interactions among genetic, environmental, and lifestyle factors that can influence long-term health and complex, chronic disease. It seemed logical to me that perhaps Wynne could be healed in mind, body, and spirit while detoxifying her body of the drugs that were killing her, thus giving her a fresh start.

We flew to San Diego, and drove the rest of the way into Mexico to start our ten-day visit. The facility was state of the art, and extremely peaceful. Again, I felt hope. This was something new that we had not thought of before, and I would be there with her to experience the detoxification process myself as well. After all, I had been drinking more lately.

The first day was full of tests and one-on-one discussions as they formalized a treatment plan for each of us. It was going to be ten days of a very strict diet (mostly juices), and a highly regulated schedule of exercise and meditation. I was very excited.

Over the next few days, we spent our free time reading and sitting by the pool when we weren't undergoing a rejuvenative treatment. Wynne seemed to be accepting the program, and at times looked happy. It was the morning of the sixth day that I woke up to find Wynne had left the complex, something that was highly discouraged not only for health reasons, as one might be tempted to stray from the diet regimen, but also for safety reasons. We were not in the best of neighborhoods outside the institute's giant gates. I found out later from the security camera tape that Wynne had walked along the wall separating the compound and the beach, and then walked through someone's yard to get out, hoping no one would see her.

I waited patiently for her to return for several hours before leaving with a few members of the staff to find her. Forty minutes into the search, the driver I was with got a call on his radio that she had come back to the facility. It turned out that she had not only made her way to the local store to get alcohol and cigarettes, but she had also managed to find a pharmacy that gave her pills! I had to admire her resourcefulness, even in the face of my utter disappointment. Needless to say, we were asked to leave, and we did. It wouldn't be the last time she left a medical facility while withdrawing from the opiates she was taking. I'm not sure we spoke again for several hours on our way home.

---

I was being pulled in so many directions by 2005 that I began to compartmentalize my time to do things for myself more often. I wish I could say that those things were all healthy choices that would make me stronger. In fact, once I made sure the kids were safe, either at school or on a sleepover at another house where adults were there to watch them, I would go out with friends just to empty my head. The things that were going on were so unbelievable that I had to talk to someone just to feel like it was real. Once the small group of fathers I had befriended in our neighborhood began to notice things weren't quite right, they became a fairly constant sounding board over several beers every few weeks. Our favorite part of the night was leaving the pub and walking to the all-night restaurant nearby to get breakfast. For a few hours, I was able to find escape in listening to the fantastic stories they would tell of their childhoods growing up in Ireland. We would talk about our lives and our kids—how we wanted to raise them, the hopes we had for them, our dreams of someday sitting on the beach in retirement with umbrellas in our drinks. I laughed until my gut hurt. Then I'd have to wake up a few hours later to get the kids to school and drive the forty miles to Menlo Park all over again.

During the first several years of Wynne's illness and our move to San Francisco, I found myself also spending more time with Wynne's cousin Denny. Not only was he a great sounding board, he had known Wynne from the time they were both in diapers. He could easily calm me down when I felt like my life was out of control, and he could motivate me when he felt I wasn't handling a particular situation as well as he would have. I can't calculate the hours we spent—and the number of Mai Tais we drank—sitting at the bar at Trader Vic's in Emeryville while I tried desperately to make sense of my life. I knew alcohol wasn't my best friend, but the time I spent with Denny is priceless to me. He was safe because he was part of the family, but he wasn't an immediate family member to Wynne so I could be open (after a few Mai Tais, as Denny would always joke). He was never surprised, nor was he judgmental, much like the many therapists whose sessions I would pay for later. In fact, the theme of nonjudgmental discourse became our mantra as a family, and I believe it ultimately helped the kids more than anything else.

There are so many regrets I have about my drinking during that period, but at the time, I thought I needed to talk to my friends, not go to a gym and work out by myself. I had to be around people who could validate my experiences and give me reasons to keep going.

In hindsight, I realize that the spring of 2005 was a major turning point for me in so many ways. My fortieth birthday came in the middle of April. Instead of looking forward to it with joy, I was filled with dread. I wanted to have a small gathering of close friends, maybe take the kids to a baseball game with some other families, but Wynne was solely focused on holding a big birthday party at the house. I think she was trying really hard to make me happy by bringing my friends, old and new, together for a big celebration. Many of my oldest friends had birthdays the same week, and she knew it. The more I protested, the more she wanted it to happen; she acted like her life almost depended on it. I probably would have felt the same way had I been having the issues she was.

I truly felt bad for her, but thought—as I had so many other times before, and would again—that having something to focus on might give her a lift. I thought that if she felt proud of what she had accomplished, she might stop what she was doing and focus on recovery. It never worked. By the time the event or project was complete, it was never as good as it had been in her mind, and the severe letdown was too much for her. It was right back to whatever part of the cycle she was in at the time.

During April 2005, it was a combination of benzodiazepines and alcohol. As her doctor-hopping behavior grew over the years, and the number of pills she was taking on a daily basis multiplied, our monthly medical and pharmaceutical drawdown surpassed $5,000. Later, the ambulance calls and subsequent emergency room visits would add up on a regular basis. The treatment facilities she entered as often as twice a year would cost a minimum of $25,000 a month on the low end, and in some cases as much as $75,000 a month. What's worse was that they all wanted to get paid *in full* before Wynne could step through the front door. It was so difficult to prepare for that huge expense because she would only agree to go if she was in the emergency room, being held on a seventy-two-hour hold. Insurance would reimburse for what they thought were "reasonable and customary" charges, but that would only be somewhere between $5,000 and $10,000 a year.

After that blowout birthday party, I began to withdraw from everyone. Not only was the party ruinous financially—it took me months to pay for—but also the way my friends looked at me with utter pity and frustration made me want to hide. I imagine Wynne felt much the same way. Wynne's substance issues had gone on for five years, and the spiral was accelerating. Everyone who knew me understood the incredible strain my family was under. It wasn't just me anymore that her behavior was affecting; the kids were now old enough to see that something wasn't right. I suspect that they knew far earlier, but now they were capable of understanding their gut feelings.

My friends had been witness to Wynne's severe decline over the past few years, and I could feel them begging me to do something—anything—different. I had absolutely no idea what to do, though. I had no control over the situation. You might think I had control over our finances or over our daily rituals with the kids, and I did. The problem, however, was that she had ways to tap into our accounts as well, and every time she made her way to another rehab facility, it would cost thousands of dollars before they would let her through the door. I was making great money, and my business was growing rapidly, but it was never enough to keep up. I had a certain arrogance that clouded my vision. I believed that no matter what she did, I could handle it eventually as my business caught up. I kept thinking that money could solve the problem. Once we found the right doctor, the right center, the right treatment plan, we'd pay whatever it took and Wynne would be cured.

Looking back, I wish I had not been making so much money because I truly believe everyone would have been better off with boundaries that I was not willing to place on the situation. If I had not had the funds to sustain Wynne's doctor-shopping or pay for help around the house, perhaps this would have ended sooner and with a better result.

# Chapter 11

# Desperation and Anger

*If you can, separate yourself from the increasing chaos to take*
*a breath and get the perspective you need to make life-changing*
*decisions. While others around you may see what's happening, it's up*
*to you to set the necessary boundaries, and make the hard choices.*

AS WE ROLLED into 2006, I was now looking at selling our house in San Francisco—a house we'd purchased—and then redone—just a few years earlier.

I had once again put significant effort into building an amazing place for the kids to enjoy as they grew up. I had again installed a basketball court, and I'd added a wall for hitting tennis balls against. There was an out-door area for the kids to ride their bikes, and an outdoor fire pit for sitting around with our friends. In the face of extreme dysfunction, the house felt like the only way to keep the appearance of normalcy not only to our friends, but to the kids who were still too young to really comprehend the gravity of the situation. If I could only keep them busy, and give them the ability to go to school without having their friends asking questions yet, I was happy.

Wynne was now very loud in voicing her objections to living in the fog belt of the city. It's true that our home was in one of San Francisco's moist-air micro-climates where bright sunlight seldom penetrated even on a sunny day. But I suspected that the real motiva-tion behind her insistence that we change neighbor-hoods was her lingering embarrassment; over the past few years, she'd been seen by friends and neighbors in varying states of obvious intoxication. That was *my* pattern. I wanted so badly to believe that a change of scenery or a project she could sink her teeth into would make her realize what she was letting slip away—her family. Looking back, however, I now believe that every time I tried to help in this regard, I only set her up for miserable disappointment. A new start can do wonders, but a moving van couldn't carry Wynne away from her issues—she brought them with her. Naturally, Wynne felt like a failure when a change of address didn't stop her old habits from reappearing, and when new friends and neighbors inevitably figured out that she was drinking and taking pills, her deepening sense of shame probably accelerated the pace of her downfall.

One spring day in 2006, I was at my desk pouring over numbers on a conference call with one of my clients. My assistant, Sandra, poked her head in. Sandra and I had worked together for over six years at this point. She was my right hand, and my clients loved her. In fact, it was her phenomenal skill set and client service acumen that allowed me to work from home as much as I did back then. She knew the firm, and the people that made it run, so well that no matter what task was at hand, she knew where to go and what to do in order to get it done with ease.

That morning, she interrupted me to say I had an urgent call about Wynne. I hastily got off the conference call. Without stopping to catch my breath, I picked up the receiver again.

"Mr. Doyle? Your wife has been in an accident." It was a police officer, calling from the scene. As I sat in my chair more than thirty-five miles away, all I could feel was immense anger. It was not the first time I'd gotten a call like this. As I hung up, I wondered if he would test Wynne for substances that would have impaired her ability to operate the car she had just plowed into the back of a parked mail truck. A few months earlier, she was sideswiped when she decided to race a MUNI train with the kids in the car.

I ran out of the office, jumped into my car, and drove to the scene of the accident at speeds greater than 90 mph. As I crested the hill on the freeway coming into San Francisco onto 19th Avenue, I realized that I had gone several miles in a complete daze. I couldn't remember the last twenty miles on the freeway. I was so busy going over different scenarios that I might be confronted with when I got to my destination that I wasn't paying any attention to my surroundings. Although the freeway I was driving on was notorious for speeding, I think I unconsciously wanted an officer to notice me so I could bring the police with me to witness what

I was going through. I had made this high-speed run several times before, however, and had never gotten pulled over. The same was true that day.

As I rolled up to the scene, I discovered Wynne had already been taken to the UCSF Medical Center for cautionary reasons after she'd slammed into the back of the mail truck.

"She seemed to be in shock," the officer informed me. His face showed compassion.

It was all I could do to hold my tongue. Of course he hadn't tested her. She had probably charmed him—and his partner, and the EMS team, and the passersby—and convinced them all that nothing was wrong. It was what she had done to me for years.

I took a deep breath. And then, as I had done so many times before, I followed Wynne's ambulance to the hospital.

Later that night, as the rain pelted our house, Wynne decided she needed to go to Walgreens a few blocks away to fill a prescription the hospital had given her. She was in her pajamas, and had clearly already taken several benzodiazepines, because she seemed to be floating through the house in her usual fog. I refused to take her, and threatened to lock her out of the house if she chose, as she had done so many other times, to leave on her own and walk there.

"You wouldn't dare!" she screamed.

"Try me," I managed to say back to her as I watched the door slam behind her. I really didn't care what she thought of me at that moment, nor did I care if she spent the night somewhere else. I wasn't going to participate in getting her more drugs. I locked the door, turned out the light, and watched through the window as she stumbled unevenly down the sidewalk in the rain.

A little more than an hour later she came home, Walgreens bag in hand. She stood outside, screaming at me to open the door. The kids were already asleep, and I was not going to go back on what I had told her in the hope that she would see that I was going to start putting boundaries in place. I really didn't want her around at that point, either. She was high on benzos, drunk, soaking wet, and angry, and her temper was on display.

The garage had been converted into a playroom for the kids, and our dog, George, a hundred-pound labradoodle, typically slept there at night. He had company that night as Wynne curled up next to him with a blanket. The next morning, I let her in.

The house sold soon after, and we moved to a different part of the city. This was our fourth move in ten years—our fifth, in fact, if you count our brief stay in a rental while we were working on the house we bought when we moved back to San Francisco. The kids were young enough that I felt it wouldn't affect them too much to change schools. I figured I could keep taking them to see their friends across town. I didn't realize it then, but this move would not be our last by a long shot. We were renting now. The instability around our housing came not only from the financial strain we were under, but the insecurity I felt about whether or not Wynne would insist on moving again. Now I see, looking back, that I still had not taken control of my situation and established boundaries that would ultimately protect us. Instead, I had begun almost taking pride in my ability to navigate chaos and all that comes with it. We were still standing, right?

Wynne was now on a cycle that brought her to the emergency room in an ambulance at least twice a year for detoxification. Each time, she'd be held for a mandatory 72 hours under Section 5150 of California's Welfare and Institutions Code, which allows a hospital to involuntarily confine a person deemed to be a danger to himself or herself by the psychiatric staff. After that, she could be kept there for up to fourteen more days, under Section 5250, for treatment of substance abuse disorder.

Then it was off to another 30-day program. This time, the hospital staff suggested we try the Hazelden inpatient addiction treatment center in Newberg, Oregon, instead of the facilities we had grown accustomed to. In the early years, we'd traveled to Southern California for treatment, but as the issue persisted, lately we found ourselves reaching out to find another solution, wherever it might be. I agreed immediately. I thought that if she spent some time away, the kids and I could regroup, and catch our breath. This would be her eighth stay in a treatment facility.

During the first week of her stay at Hazelden, one of my best friends committed suicide. He was one of the guys I went out with from the other side of town where we had moved from just recently. It wasn't just the fact that he had hung himself that pushed me over the edge; it was that he had young kids who were best friends with my kids. It also broke me to hear that he had actually sat down and thought about it while puffing on a cigarette, and then still did it. The degree of pain he must have felt consumed me. I was devastated. I couldn't function, but I still had responsibilities—the kids, and their school, and my work. I must have sat outside in my backyard for hours, tears streaming down my face as I lamented my friend's death and my own pitiful situation. I wondered if I was capable of doing the same thing. The more I thought about his pain, the more everything else I was feeling came to the surface.

I was experiencing a full-blown emotional crisis. I called my doctor and she made an appointment with a psychiatrist. I was in his office an hour later, still incapable of speaking. I left a few hours later with a prescription for Valium. The irony of this was not lost on me, but I saw no other option. For the first time in my life, I thought I was literally falling apart. I had no middle ground emotionally. I was seesawing wildly between raw emotional pain and a state of complete numbness, without any feeling.

Before I took any pills, though, I decided to pile the kids into the car and drive to Los Angeles to stay for a while with my brother Bill and his family. I sat on his couch for the next few days, and I'm embarrassed to say that I don't remember a thing. Valium is the scariest thing I had ever taken. I had absolutely no memory. Bill told me later that we just played video games with the kids and watched movies. I woke up on the third day there, feeling as though I'd survived the immediate crisis but lost two days in my memory bank, and drove home. I had no idea Valium could do that, but maybe that's one of the wanted effects in situations that are so intense and troubling that you need to check out. I have never taken Valium since.

Seeing my brother and his wife, who had her own issues with substance abuse—issues that would ultimately drive them apart as well—made me wonder about learned cycles that we fall into subconsciously. My father's parents both suffered from alcoholism. His mother passed away at age forty-nine, and his father died just a few years later. My mother's only two brothers— my uncles—both died young from severe alcohol-related illnesses, too. I don't recall either of my own parents having a drinking issue. In fact, they were completely intolerant of my brother and me experimenting with alcohol when we were teenagers and young adults. I'm guessing that was mostly out of fear, and rightly so. The question I have is how both my brother and I could marry women who would ultimately develop substance abuse issues to the point that they would each lose custody of their children, and one of them would even lose her life. I have worked incredibly hard to make sure my kids recognize patterns in their choices throughout their lives in hopes that they can break this cycle.

Another week went by, and then it was Family Week at Hazelden. My sadness had morphed into red-hot anger. The kids were in school, so I went up to Oregon alone. You could instantly tell this wasn't my first "family week," as I arrived two days late, with a massive chip on my shoulder for having to be there at all. Nothing else had worked. Why in the hell would this?

"Hello, Britt. We've been expecting you. Thank you for joining us." The group facilitator was bubbly and enthusiastic. I figured she had to be, given the fear and confusion she likely saw in the eyes of almost everyone who had come there to understand and share experiences.

I took a seat in the front. No one in these uncomfortable situations likes to sit in front, I remember thinking. You don't want to feel on the spot; you're there to hear from other people and feel you aren't alone. I just wanted to numb out and stop thinking, but the only remaining seats were in the front row. A young woman continued the discussion that was going on before I arrived. I don't really remember the topic; only that she had such a hopeful tone in her voice. She was there for her boyfriend, and she wanted everyone to know she was committed. The darkness I was feeling finally spilled out like black tar as I spoke up and delivered what I thought was sound advice:

"Run away," I said slowly, enunciating every syllable. "It doesn't get any better. I *can't* leave. I have three little kids. If I leave and don't get full custody, my kids will be living in danger. But you—what the hell are you thinking?!"

It was one of the ugliest things I've ever said to anyone. I literally saw no way out. I was solely focused now on keeping the kids safe and restoring order to my life somehow.

If all of this weren't enough, within a few months after Wynne had completed that detox program, my aunt Susie, my mother's sister, called to tell me that her husband, my uncle Alan, a man who had been a strong positive presence in my life, was in his last few days of his battle with cancer. I was coming out of a movie with the kids when I got the call. I must have gone white because the kids were immediately on high alert. They had, unfortunately, developed a hypersensitivity to emotions in our house. We all had. Looking for clues from Wynne as to how the day was going to go was critical to survival in our constantly changing ecosystem. One day she would be lucid and engaging. Another day would see her drift in and out of consciousness. Still other days would start with her taking a walk, only to end up passed out by 10:00 a.m. We never knew what was coming, but we were learning to read the cues.

Alan and Susie moved to California around the same time my own family did, in the early 1970s. They set a great example of living life without judgment. Alan was a master carpenter who could build stunning custom cabinetry for the most opulent houses you could imagine. He was also a musician, and played the harmonica—the mouth harp—with several famous bands, including Three Dog Night, Canned Heat, Janis Joplin, and Taj Mahal. He brought the house down once when Susie and I were with him in the Boom Boom Room, a divey San Francisco blues club. That happened right before I met Wynne. I only saw Alan play live a few times in my life, and they were very special. When I was growing up, Alan gave me a sense of calm that no one else had done to that point. I still try to incorporate his mindset into my everyday life. So the news of his illness came as a blow.

I got my in-laws to watch the kids, and hopped on an airplane a few hours later, Wynne in tow. As we reached my uncle's side, I was filled with immense gratitude that I was able to be there with him, and with Susie and her daughter, my cousin Samara. In my mind, they were the model for a kind and loving relationship. I wished that Wynne would see the bond they had, recognize how fleeting our lives are, and recommit to beating this substance abuse disorder she was battling. Writing this now, I can see how ridiculous my thoughts were. By trying to get Wynne to see how wonderful life was, all I was really doing was making her feel worse! My misguided attempts to make her realize what she was doing were simply feeding the wrong beast.

Brannon tells a story in kenpo class about how we each have two dogs inside of us. One is red, and the other blue. The red one is the bad dog that makes us do the things that will harm us, and the blue dog is the good dog that makes us healthy and prosperous. Whichever one we feed will obviously get stronger. We need to make a conscious decision to feed the blue dog every day to keep the red one at bay, and eventually see it wither away.

I was able to be with Alan for the last few hours of his life. He asked if we would roll his wheelchair onto the front lawn, which we did. We spent his final hour talking to him while he ran his feet back and forth on the grass and stared at the sun, tears rolling down his cheeks. I'll never forget feeling like I had to concentrate to take every breath as I watched him fold into himself.

At Alan's funeral, more than five hundred people invaded the freeways on motorcycles and in cars to follow his casket to the Celebration of Life ceremony that had been planned. Although my family members were there, I had suddenly never felt so alone. It was as if every ounce of air had left my body, and I was deflating completely. I sat looking at his pictures, and listening to others talk about what an amazing musician, father, and friend he was, and I simply felt done. I wanted to get up and speak to everyone assembled there about how he had touched my life, but I literally couldn't even stand up. It was as if I had been swept up in a massive tidal wave, and was being pummeled along the sand underneath as I gasped for air. It was paralyzing.

Alan's death was indeed a very sad event for me, and for those close to him. For me, it was really the final insult in what was already an extraordinary time in my life; I can honestly say I was as close to giving up as I could possibly be. The thought of my kids was the only thing at that point that kept me fighting. Imagine holding in your emotions in order to keep moving forward, and then something occurs, like the loss of a loved one, that gives you permission to let your feelings out—but your feelings are too painful, so you try to stuff them back inside. Too late!

---

It was a few months later that I began to really focus on the mental health of the kids. They were old enough by that time, and had seen enough, to be told the truth. We began seeing a counselor together. I would use this episode when my emotions were truly uncontrollable to emphasize the need for them to address their fears and questions now rather than letting them stay bottled up. Taking them to counseling was the best decision I ever made for them. Trying to protect them from the emotions they were obviously feeling wasn't an option anymore. The crazy thing was, however, that over the next several years, I would continue to try to protect them from information and life decisions that I felt would make them sad, ultimately putting us all in a very precarious financial position.

# Chapter 12

# Permission

*Money is not the cure,*
*especially when you need it.*

IN THE SPRING of 2007, I received a call that would change my life profoundly. I had spent the last ten years of my professional life working for an extremely successful branch of Citigroup's Family Office division, helping some of Silicon Valley's wealthiest entrepreneurs invest their fortunes. My office was located on

Sand Hill Road in Menlo Park, arguably the epicenter of new wealth creation on the planet. As a very successful wealth advisor, I was a "hot commodity," and I received calls from recruiters on a regular basis. They were all the same: "We represent a client looking for talented brokers to hire. They're writing big checks, and you fit what they're looking for." I was happy where I was, however. I had a great manager, a great relationship with the senior advisor in the office, and a great team.

This call was different, though. It was intriguing because the recruiter had done her homework on my business, and knew the specific training I had received. She knew what my business model was. The caller described an opportunity to build a new offering for a large international investment bank looking to make a splash in the US ultra-high net worth private client market. She explained that I would be one of fewer than twenty team leaders brought into the bank's San Francisco office to deliver customized solutions to families with $25 million or more in assets to invest. The San Francisco office would be one of eight nationwide. The firm was UBS. Headquartered in Basel, Switzerland, UBS was one of the world's most prestigious private banks. It catered to the most affluent families in Europe.

This was an opportunity worthy of further consideration, and perhaps one that could even provide a way out of my financial woes.

UBS and I courted for over a year as I continued to focus on work and the kids. The stock market had begun to fluctuate wildly, but I proceeded on the assumption that it would settle down soon. By this point, unfortunately, I had resigned myself to the fact that I believed Wynne would never get better. I still cared deeply for her, and had incredible sympathy for what she was going through, but I just couldn't be part of it anymore. I couldn't leave her, though, because I was afraid I wouldn't get full custody of the kids—and the kids were still too young to be alone with her if I didn't. Wynne was gifted at acting the part of the wonderful, doting mother when she wanted to do so—even though it was a complete illusion. She worked on her public image, even trying with the help of some terrific friends to get involved with various groups like the Opera Guild and the Board of Directors of the San Francisco Symphony. She was never able to follow through. I truly felt for her, but nothing she did was in my control, ever.

The summer of 2008 started off with us in Lake Tahoe at her family's house. The kids and I spent most of our time there on or near the water, enjoying family and friends who were visiting there as well. Wynne was now having a really difficult time being around almost everyone, because she thought they were judging her. They were. We all were. In our minds, she had never admitted there was a problem, and that was what made us all angry. If she had admitted it, we all would have encircled and embraced her. Maybe she knew that, and couldn't bear it.

A few weeks later, while at home, she was taken away in an ambulance for the last time that I was together with her. After her mandatory hospital stay, she flew to Los Angeles to undergo detox at Passages Malibu, another luxury addiction treatment center. It was late June 2008. She had not wanted me to go with her, so I obliged. The first thing I did, however, was cut off her credit cards. I didn't want another situation where she disappeared into the LA motel scene and we couldn't find her.

I was right to be concerned. After stepping off the plane in Los Angeles, she went directly to an ATM, where she discovered she was unable to withdraw any money. She spotted the driver from Passages and started running away and screaming at the top of her lungs.

"He's trying to kill me! Somebody call 911!"

I was on the phone with the Passages director of admissions, who had the driver on another line. It was a scene out of the movie *Catch Me If You Can!* The director lamented that they would likely not be able to take her because of the severe nature of the situation. After all, they really only take people who want to be there to get help.

Agents from the Department of Homeland Security circled Wynne and the driver, guns drawn, while I was on the phone with the director of admissions, and he was on the phone with the driver. The driver handed the phone to the man in charge, who let them go after listening to several minutes of explanation. My only words to the people at Passages were that I wasn't coming to get Wynne, and as I had already paid the first monthly fee of $75,000 to get her admitted, she was their problem.

It's a good thing the director of Passages talked the authorities into bringing her to the facility. The doctors there told me later that in the state she was in, she would have died from withdrawal if she'd been taken into custody.

"Will you be joining us for the family week events next week?" asked one of the Passages founders.

"No," I replied. "I've been to so many of them in the past, I could run the discussion groups myself. I'm not sure I or anyone else will get anything out of my being there. Besides, I have to take care of the kids." I remember that moment so clearly. I was walking through the middle of Union Square, looking up at the sky, and trying to catch my breath as I spoke to him. The anxiety was overwhelming.

"Sounds like you've had enough," he said.

"Yes, you could say that," I countered. "I think I've definitely paid my dues." As the years went by, as horrible as this sounds, I grew to crave the times Wynne was gone. The kids and I needed the space to take a breath.

I'd had this sort of conversation before. This time was different, though.

"If you're going to file for divorce, you should do it while she's here, so we can work through it in a safe environment rather than having her come home and have to deal with the repercussions by herself. We can help her better while she's here."

My God, I thought, this is the first time anyone has given me *permission!* Leaving this horrible situation wasn't unthinkable; it was actually something I could consider. Without stopping to frame my reply, I shot back: "Then yes, I am going to file for divorce."

It was an extremely difficult decision. What I didn't account for was the ferocity with which Wynne would fight for custody rights. I didn't want to keep the children from her completely, but their safety came first. I spent the time and money to keep them safe. I had no choice.

According to many health advocates, the top five stress-inducing events that can put us at risk are the death of a loved one, divorce, moving, major illness, and job loss. In the space of the next two months, I filed for divorce, moved from San Francisco across the Golden Gate Bridge to Marin County, and left a stable job that I loved.

Although these back-to-back changes were stressful, they were necessary. I was upending my world, but I thought I would soon get my bearings and life would improve for me and for the kids.

# Chapter 13

# Upheaval

*Living with a substance abuser, you tend to get numb.*
*Don't be afraid when you start to feel alive again.*
*It's almost like having frostbite: an object at room temperature*
*feels normal to everyone else, but to you, it's scalding hot.*

THE MOVE FROM San Francisco to Marin occurred suddenly, with one quick phone call to my friend Tom McCarthy, who had moved us twice already, and would move us again four more times over the next eight years.

I found a beautiful little house in Marin backing up to a hill so that it felt hidden, quiet, and safe. At this point, I was not thinking about Wynne anymore. I loaded the van with half the furniture and kitchen appliances, and the kids and I were gone. Although Passages offered her a second month of addiction treatment for free, Wynne ran out the door when her month was up. She came home to what must have been a devastating scene; her children and her husband gone. As much as I felt for her, I couldn't live with her anymore.

Panic in the markets was starting to set in at a terrific pace. March 2008 saw the near collapse and subsequent bailout of Bear Stearns. The markets then calmed down for a few weeks, but by May they were swinging wildly. In a shocking move, Lehman Brothers filed for Chapter 11 bankruptcy protection on September 15. This was the largest bankruptcy filing in US history, and it put extreme stress on already volatile markets. During the months leading up to October 2008, it was not unusual for the markets to move 5 to 10 percent up or down in a single day. On September 29, the Dow plunged 777 points, its largest point drop on record. On October 13, it gained 936 points, its biggest one-day gain on record.

I was getting intense pressure from several clients at this point as well, wondering if Citigroup, the firm I worked for—and that held their investments—was going to survive, and if not, what would happen to their money. There was a clear sense of panic setting in. Someone even asked me if I had heard that banks were going to shut down ATM activity. These are the times CNBC lives for! What better reason to watch CNBC than to scare yourself to death.

When a wealth advisor chooses to leave a firm to work for a competitor, there are certain agreed-upon industry protocols that must be adhered to by that advisor with respect to the client base he or she has been servicing. I used to tell my kids that they could picture my role as something like that of a baseball player on a team who might eventually play well enough to get a large contract from an opposing team. The only difference was that I needed to be able to convince my clients that I had brought to the firm to move with me.

Under the protocol, advisors are prohibited from telling clients that they are contemplating moving to another firm. Further, they are prohibited from taking financial information with them. On the other hand, advisors are expected to walk in to their manager's office the day they are to leave, and resign on the spot, with a list of clients they intend to pursue in hand. At that moment, the manager will discuss any final issues outstanding, and the advisor travels to his or her new office to begin the task of convincing clients to move, too.

Easier said than done, I found out.

In the midst of this uncertain economic situation, I continued my negotiations to relocate to UBS. I got together several times with the office manager for the San Francisco office of the new division I would be joining. I gave her my production and asset numbers and my projected figures to help her understand the revenue and asset goals I felt I could accomplish. It was important that no one at Citi knew of my plans until I was ready to reveal them, so she and I met outside our respective offices, at coffee houses and restaurants. It felt as if I were having an affair, my spouse being my colleagues and coworkers at the office.

I gave her a list of accounts and the asset mixes, without divulging my clients' names. We discussed which accounts were likely to move to UBS; which accounts held assets in simple stocks, bonds, and cash; and which accounts were committed to alternative investments that might not be able to move because UBS hadn't approved them. Proprietary alternative investments such as hedge funds, private equity, real estate, and venture capital were some of the differentiating factors for a wealthy family to choose an investment banking relationship. Every firm took pride in offering what they considered "best of breed" for every investment theme.

As we were talking, she described many comforting allowances she was going to make based on the type of assets my clients owned. Due to the illiquid nature of some of the assets, and the fact that many of the investment management firms I was partnering with to manage client money did not have a relationship with UBS, she would not count a portion toward my measure of success if we were unable to bring them to the firm. Essentially, I was going to have to establish new relationships with UBS-approved money managers, and reallocate the clients who moved their accounts to UBS with me into these new strategies.

She and I met several times over a two-month period to hash out a deal. I flew to New York to meet management as well as the stock option administration team. I thought I had done as much due diligence as was humanly possible, and more importantly, I believed that UBS wanted to build something better than the competition. It's easy to rationalize and only see the good parts when you're about to sell your soul to the devil.

It was October 24, 2008. I was alone in my house with my three kids. It was a Friday morning, and the market had already dropped close to 500 points. CNBC's usual doomsday prognosticators were warning anyone who would listen that we were far from the bottom. My clients should be calling the office or my cell phone wanting to speak to me for reassurance that we had made the correct decisions with their holdings. Why wasn't my BlackBerry ringing? I reached for my phone to check in with my team, but the phone didn't show any missed calls. Instead, there was a message on the screen asking if I wanted to start the setup process.

My heart started pounding, and I realized I was sweating. I remember a distinct ringing in my ears as well. I was completely cut off from my clients and my support team at the office. I had forgotten to turn my phone off, and to my utter shock, the management team had remotely wiped my phone clean before I could do a thing about it! I had not figured into the equation that my manager had anticipated my departure to the day. To make things worse, I had not planned ahead to have someone with me to take the kids to school. I was usually in the office by 6:00 a.m. (the stock markets open on the west coast at 6:30), but on that particular day, my manager and his staff had several hours to thwart my attempts to move my clients before I even had a chance to resign. I had once again been too trusting. I was standing in the middle of the kitchen with my kids—ages eight, ten, and eleven—staring at me fearfully, wondering why I had turned so pale.

"Hey, Dad, is your company's stock falling so much because you're not going to be there anymore?"

This was the greatest thing Preston had ever asked me. I immediately felt more at ease. *This* was why I needed to succeed, I thought. My kids believed in me, and I wasn't going to let them down. I was going to work for UBS, and we were going to be fine. I had just split from their mother, and moved them out of our home. In my mind, they didn't deserve to be affected by further misfortune.

We were living in Marin, more than an hour's drive from my Menlo Park office, and I still had to get the kids to school before I could go into the office and resign in person to my good friend and manager, Guy. Suddenly, a piercing ring from the home phone, which we never used, jolted me back to reality. It was Sandra, my assistant. I had relied on her heavily to keep my business in order for years. She could anticipate a client's needs, and most importantly, she *never* said no to a client unless we had exhausted *every* angle. She was a major reason for my success. Clients loved her.

Now, she was on the other end of the line, crying so hard I couldn't understand her. She had been escorted out of the office like a common criminal. Management had, indeed, been watching the activity in my operation, and had been waiting for this day. There I was, standing in my kitchen with my three kids, no cell phone, no one to answer my work phone except the vultures (people I'd thought of as colleagues and friends yesterday) who would ultimately steal my clients, and no way of communicating with *anyone* once I left the house. I was completely fucked. Yet I still needed to get the last of my personal items from my office at Citigroup, and resign according to the rules of the broker protocol.

The drive to school was a complete blur. I was definitely not thinking clearly, and I don't even remember dropping off the kids. The next memory I have is of driving on Interstate 280 at over 80 miles per hour. Once again, my life was in chaos mode, but this time it was my business life. As I mentioned before, I had always thought of my life as a three-legged stool, the legs being health, money, and home. Now the one leg I thought was the most stable was cracking. Soon I'd be sitting on the floor.

As I approached my office, I could see Sandra and my junior partner, Gary, waiting on the steps outside, looking completely beaten. The management team must have been watching from inside the office because as I sped through the parking lot toward the entrance, Guy appeared through the double doors, and walked toward my car. "I'm really sorry to see you go, and even sorrier for the way this morning is going for you." I knew he genuinely meant it. We were friends. I had taken him out several times in San Francisco when he was recruited to run our office nearly nine years earlier.

He was not only aware of my tenuous situation at home, but also had signed off on the loan I had recently taken out. The loan, backed by my business partner Andy's assets, was what enabled me to continue paying for the medical treatment Wynne was getting and stay afloat despite some other unfortunate financial decisions I'd made. On the other hand, it meant I was in massive debt. Guy knew the pressure I was under, both financially and from my clients. We had grown close over the years as we gained a mutual trust and respect for each other. I mention this because even though the morning I left was incredibly stressful and the actions taken by Guy and the rest of the advisors in my office had a significant negative impact on my ability to retain my client base, I know that they were all simply doing what every other manager and advisor pool would do to another advisor leaving the firm. I was simply naïve to think my colleagues at the office would treat me as a friend—as I think I would have treated them if they were transferring to another firm. Instead, I was being treated like a threat, or even a traitor.

Guy, who remains a close friend, took me to breakfast across the street to discuss next steps, which he couched as simply his duty as manager of the office and nothing personal. He wished me well, and we parted. I was extremely anxious to get to UBS to start my new position—that very morning. I needed to connect with my clients as soon as possible and salvage my relationships with them. As soon as Guy and I finished our conversation, I headed into San Francisco. My new office was in the Bank of America Building at 555 California Street, on the 32nd floor.

As I entered the building, I was greeted by my new manager and the assistants who would set up my operations and office. Sandra and Gary were already there, having headed over while I met with Guy. I was escorted to the manager's office to officially sign the contract and start the process of sending out packets to my clients. They put in an order for me to get a new BlackBerry, too! What a relief. It had been years since I had been out of touch with the world like this.

Ironically, I had actually started my career at Kidder, Peabody eighteen years earlier, and their offices were in this very building—in fact, on this very floor! Kidder was bought by Paine Webber, which in turn was bought by UBS. They'd completely renovated the space and I had an amazing office looking out at Alcatraz Island. The floor-to-ceiling internal glass walls would turn opaque with the flip of a switch. As I looked around at the magnificent offices lining the corridor, I remember thinking that I had definitely made a major decision, and there was no turning back. It's an understatement to say I was excited, but at the same time, I was incredibly nervous.

I had to live up to expectations. I knew I belonged there, but I was now out of my comfort zone that I had created over many years with my friends and colleagues at Citigroup.

What I didn't fully understand that day was that my lack of communication with my clients on that day—a day of dropping stock prices and deepening fears of recession—was unacceptable. Even more important to them was my furtiveness about my plans to leave Citi and join UBS. Because I followed the broker protocol, my clients were caught by surprise, and surprises were unwelcome in that unsettled economic climate. Many of my clients had their corporate stock plan accounts at Citigroup along with other investments they couldn't disturb. It was not in their best interests to move their assets to another investment bank just to follow a guy who had left them out to dry during an incredibly difficult market. At any other office, my departure would have been easier for me; it would have been seen as an acceptable risk for me to take, given the large size and complicated nature of my business, but we had several of Citi's top one hundred advisors in the entire firm working alongside me in that office. Even though I had what I thought were great relationships with my clients and their families, those other advisors were very good at what they did, and ultimately they managed to convince most of my clients to stay at Citigroup until the storm was over. They ended up staying for good after that. Guy had already divided my accounts up among the investment managers. They'd analyzed the investments that each client owned and were ready to talk about their current portfolios, as well as what changes they would make. That's an easy discussion when your prospect is losing money!

I should have been much more cautious, but I didn't think anyone at Citi would really try to keep my clients because they all knew what was happening in my personal and financial life. We were not just colleagues there at Citi, we were friends.

When my manager handed me accounts after an advisor left, my standard line to the clients was, "I want you to know that I'm here to service your account in the event you'd like to stay, but I realize this is a very personal business. Please let me know if I can help transition you to your advisor's new firm if that's what you'd like to do." I thought there was a code of sorts. That code actually only existed in my head, apparently.

Even though I had a substantial business in terms of revenue and assets, there were still four advisors in my Citi office who were bigger revenue-generators, and five more who were right behind me and just as hungry. I would probably have had a better chance of bringing my clients over to UBS with me if I had been the biggest moneymaker in the office because no one would be able to match my abilities, but in this case, my colleagues were all as capable of discussing financial goals, limitations, and strategy with my clients as I was. I respected everyone in my office. We were all good at what we did, and we had all been trained the same way.

# Chapter 14

# Taking Control

## MY TOWN

*The ocean tide that I see every day,*
*Reminds me of my home in the beautiful bay.*
*The friendly neighbors at every door,*
*The warm sunny days that are never a bore.*

*I live in the pink house just to the right,*
*With the dog that's all bark, but never a bite.*
*The big tall windows where light shines through,*
*And my family coming and going always with something to do.*

*It's usually quite peaceful, there isn't much noise . . .*
*Except for the fact that I live with four boys.*

*Holidays are the best when you live in my town,*
*There are decorations everywhere and the lights are hardly down.*

*I hope to stay in this town awhile,*
*It's one of the main things that really makes me smile.*

—K. BRITT DOYLE (Little Britt), age ten

A FEW MONTHS EARLIER, as I was moving into the small house in Marin with the kids, I met a woman who made me feel as if I'd been shot out of a cannon. Her name was Truth. Our mutual friends, Peter and Catrina, brought us both to Napa to spend the afternoon and have dinner together. It was a setup, but very casual. They knew us both, and knew we would at least like each other and enjoy a festive outing. We locked eyes as I walked into the pool area where Truth and Catrina were sipping on margaritas. Immediately, I got that feeling you get when you think you've known someone forever and they're meant to play a part in the story of your life. It's only in hindsight that you come to understand just how large that part may be.

Everything about Truth calmed me down. She had the ability to help me see things with more compassion. She had a two-year-old son, Julian, too. (He is the "fourth boy" in Little Britt's poem at the front of this chapter.) Truth and I were both parents—and we both knew we wanted to prioritize the kids in our relationship. It was never a question. Being at her apartment in the Sausalito hills overlooking the San Francisco Bay was like taking a vacation. Every time I walked through the door, I took a deep breath, and left the anxiety outside. She would let me just melt into a chair with a glass of wine while she cooked dinner, and we talked about work. It was "adult" time; we were carrying on the conversations normal adults do. It may sound like a small thing, but to me it was so refreshing.

Soon I was happy and having fun. Even though I did feel guilty for "abandoning" Wynne, given everything I'd been working through with her the past several years, I felt I actually deserved to be happy. Some would say it was too soon to get involved with someone else, but actually, my relationship with Wynne had been failing for many years. As wonderful as she had been at one point, Wynne had become a burden and the source of massive anxiety for me and for our kids. By the time I moved out, our friends had begun to stop calling, and I was taking the kids out of the house for dinner most nights so that they didn't have to see her passed out in bed.

I had been in therapy for a few years at that point, and had attended several family weeks at different treatment facilities where Wynne was staying. At one point, during a session a few months after I moved to Marin, my therapist remarked that it was odd that I knew where Wynne was and what she was doing seemingly at all times, even though we were no longer together. I had become hypersensitive to her state of mind, to the point that it became something I couldn't control. I told myself I was only concerned for the safety of the kids, but it was my sickness. It was almost as if we were still together, still connected, even though I couldn't stand what she had become.

At this time, the lines became blurred between what made good sense for the safety of the kids and Wynne's needs and right to see them. Because my oldest, Preston, was eleven years old and had owned his own cell phone for four years already, I thought that the kids would be okay alone with her for short periods of time if I thought she was sober. I knew I could tell right away if she had taken pills or been drinking so I allowed the kids to see her without me, reasoning that they would have the ability to make a phone call to me if they were in trouble. I knew they wanted to see their mother, and she wanted to see them, so if they were safe in my opinion, then that's what occurred.

At first, that policy seemed to be working out for everyone in the family, but occasionally the kids would come home with upsetting stories. Gradually, I recognized that they were experiencing more severe emotional strain than I first acknowledged. It wasn't the stories they told me as much as it was the stories I realized they weren't telling me. They truly wanted to see their mother, obviously—but not this way.

By now, I had been granted temporary sole custody of the children based on what was in their best interests while Wynne and I negotiated a divorce. Wynne and her family were fighting furiously with me in court to gain back her custody rights so she could have the kids at least half the time. When she was denied and I stopped allowing the kids to be with her as often, she fell into the deepest hole she had been in to date.

Christmas morning came, and I brought the kids to see Wynne at her apartment. She had called me the night before, and pleaded with me to bring the kids over for the day, telling me in great detail about the lengths she had gone to in order to make this Christmas special for them. I agreed to bring them only if her parents would be there.

The kids were very excited to spend the holiday with their mother. They were up early and dressed to go by 7:00 a.m. We rang the doorbell half an hour later with great anticipation, only to have Wynne answer the door in a dress and heels, completely incapacitated. She could barely walk, and had clearly been crying, judging from the black waterfalls running down her cheeks. I was anticipating her not being at her best, but this was unbearable. The kids raced to give her a hug, and then ran over to the Christmas tree to look at the decorations and presents as I sat there with my heart racing, as had been the situation so many times before, wondering how long I was going to let the kids stay.

A few minutes later, Wynne's parents arrived. They looked crushed as they walked through the door and saw her barely able to sit up on the couch next to the kids. Her father took me into the other room to try to convince me to leave the kids and go home, but as we were speaking, I heard Wynne's mother yelling at her in the living room. I made the decision to take the kids back home with me. I still believe that was the right decision. The trauma of seeing their mother like that on Christmas morning (or any morning, for that matter), and the knowledge that I could deliberately allow them to stay around her when she was in that state, seemed worse to me than taking them away from her that day.

I piled the kids in the car with Truth and her son, and we drove to Humboldt to spend Christmas with Truth's family. It was the first time the kids were able to spend time with Gramma Mo, Truth's mom. This was the beginning of a relationship that would grow exponentially over the next several years, as she became a sounding board for the kids outside of their normal circles of family, friends, and therapists. She had wisdom and understanding that came from experience and love.

Bayside Marin Treatment Center in San Rafael was Wynne's next stop a few days later. I was no longer willing to participate wholly in her addiction treatment, although she was still covered by my health insurance plan, for her sake. Of course, despite that, the treatment centers, as ineffective as they were for her, were always very expensive. At least this time she would be close to the kids, so that I wouldn't have to drive them as far for weekend visits.

She was released in early February, and struggled to regain her footing again alone in her San Francisco apartment.

It wasn't more than few months later that Wynne slammed into the back of a parked garbage truck at 5:45 in the morning. She was on her way to the store, with a .34 blood alcohol level. Wynne was taken to the emergency room in an ambulance again after they determined at the accident scene that she'd ingested a deadly mixture of pills and alcohol. I got a call from the hospital asking if I had the kids with me. She was trying to get out of another 72-hour involuntary confinement by claiming that she couldn't leave her kids alone. "Please don't take me away from the kids," she mumbled to the nurse. Even though I assured the woman on the phone that I had them safely with me, I received a call from Child Protective Services that very next morning.

It was the first time, but I had been waiting for years to hear from them. I remember feeling cold, and very light-headed as I listened to the social worker explain the steps she would need to take given the severe nature of the problem. Among the many forms I had to fill out and the interviews I had to endure, the one thing that scared me the most was her call to the kids' school. I think it was so unnerving because now outsiders were involved in decisions concerning the children.

Wynne spent the next few days in the hospital undergoing medical detoxification. The kids and I visited her after school on her second day there. I left the kids with her at the hospital, and went to her apartment a few blocks away to feed the cat. It was the first time I'd seen the inside of her place since she moved there. As I walked through the front hall toward the kitchen, I was shocked to find she'd covered an entire wall with pictures of our family over the years. There must have been at least five hundred photographs, all taped together like a sheet of wallpaper. I couldn't stop staring at them. The pain she must have felt putting those pictures together in that way was stunning. I felt such extreme guilt for leaving, but I still knew I had done the right thing for the kids and myself. I reminded myself that Wynne had not ever admitted to having a problem. It was shocking.

This time her father got involved, and convinced her to check herself into Narconon of Northern California, a drug rehabilitation center in Watsonville, where she remained for the next year. All court proceedings were put on hold, and I felt some sense of peace as my life seemed to slow down, and retake the shape one would normally expect, with sports and functions at the kids' schools, and recovering my own identity. I knew the kids were safe, and I didn't have to make the daily choice to let them see her. I felt that Wynne was finally doing something that would turn her situation around. By the time she left the program, she looked and sounded like the Wynne we all knew. Maybe she had been able to confront her demons at last.

"Whatever you're doing at Narconon, it's really working!" I exclaimed.

I was hopeful again for the first time in a long time. My relationship with Wynne had been burned beyond repair, but the kids needed her to be their mother, and Wynne needed that for herself. Unfortunately, her desire to get custody of the kids again was so overwhelming, especially because of the time she had lost, that it became toxic. Fighting to regain custody was extremely stressful and Wynne was unable to keep her sobriety for long. What had worked for her was changing her environment completely.

At Narconon, she was surrounded by good people who encouraged her, and helped her to rebuild her self-esteem. Stepping out of that environment and moving back to San Francisco to see the kids more often undermined all the work she had done there. In just a few short months, she was struggling with drugs and alcohol again.

Now that she was back, the custody and alimony disputes that had been on hold finally landed in court. I had been granted full custody when I filed for divorce many months before, but now we were going to determine who would have legal custody of the kids going forward.

Instead of trying to work through a solution that would be best for the kids, Wynne tried to convince the judge that I was unfit, and that she needed to have full custody. To my dismay, the judge issued an order for me to have a custody evaluator invade our lives for the next six months, at a cost of close to $50,000. This court-appointed evaluator must have interviewed nearly everyone that had come in contact with the kids over the past few years. His report was over seventy pages long. At the end, he concluded that I should maintain full custody in the short term, while he outlined the several steps that Wynne must take in order to "earn" her way to sharing custody jointly with me. These included agreeing to wear a SCRAM ankle bracelet. These devices continuously monitor the wearer's perspiration to detect even minute levels of alcohol in the body. The results are sent to a local monitoring service that notifies the appropriate authorities if the person's sweat contains alcohol or if the bracelet has been tampered with. She was also asked to install a car ignition Breathalyzer so that the car would not start if she had been drinking. She was to consent to random drug testing and weekly behavioral counseling. Wynne grudgingly agreed to all of this. At the same time, she made the decision not to speak to me again because I was finally enforcing rational actions to keep the kids safe.

We were able to finalize the divorce, finally, but the judge ordered me to pay a massive monthly alimony check. He based the amount on what I was making before Wynne and I split—before 2008, before I lost my Citi clients. In addition, I took responsibility for all other community debt, the term used in California courts for debt that either partner incurs during the course of the marriage, even if only one spouse signed the paperwork. Wynne and I were in debt to the tune of $3.8 million, a staggering figure. I felt confident, however, that I could pay it down quickly by building my business back up to the level it had been in the past.

I wasn't the only one in this situation, either. Many others in the financial industry lost their jobs in 2008 but were still saddled with large court-ordered alimony and child support payments based on their pre-2008 earnings—before they were fired or lost their jobs because their companies failed. Some states had laws on the books that made alimony determinations permanent, whether or not the breadwinner's economic circumstances changed. I read a news account of one man who was jailed eight times for missing alimony payments. He was a high-earning portfolio manager until the financial crisis of 2008, when he lost his job and used up his savings. Nonetheless, he continued to owe his ex-wife $78,000 a year in alimony. In my case, the figure was closer to $175,000 a year!

I would have been able to sustain the alimony payments I owed had I not used the majority of my hiring incentive bonus to pay off the debt we had accumulated while we were married. Once that bonus money was gone, I was going into further debt to maintain alimony payments and my own household. Oddly, I was not bitter . . . yet. I arrogantly continued to believe I had the ability to "out-earn" the situation. I truly wanted Wynne to succeed, so she could reenter society and our kids' lives again. If she could only do that with the help of the money I was ordered to give her, then I was okay with providing that financial support. The problem was that nothing changed; Wynne still had not fully committed to her sobriety. She was so defiant! She felt she had been cured, and there was no longer an issue.

Truth and I had now been together for a little over eighteen months. Not only had she kept me strong and focused, but also she was constantly there to pick up the pieces when the kids came home from seeing their mother. It broke both of our hearts seeing their sadness, disappointment, and longing for their mother to "get better." Truth's compassion was unlike anything I had ever experienced. It was intoxicating. I wanted so badly to be able to make everything right, to fix everything. Chaos had played such a prominent role in my life, and the kids' lives, for so long that I really hadn't considered the effect it was starting to have on Truth. It was, still, only going to get worse.

Truth kept a diary at times so that we would have notes to remind us of details during custody hearings. I think she also needed to write things down to help her process what was happening around her. What had become "normal" for me was shocking and traumatic to her. The following pages cover a two-month period in February and March 2009 when Wynne returned from a month at Bayside Marin, another "luxury" substance abuse treatment center.

## Excerpts from Truth's Journal

2/6 — Released from Bayside

Week of 2/9 — Seems to being doing good

Week of 2/16 — We are in Cabo. By Wed. 2/18 Britt notices slurring on phone as well as Hilary and kids. [Hilary was one of Wynne's best friends. She called us and said she had noticed Wynne slurring after having a conversation with her.]

2/18 — She erupts when Michele & Collette aren't able to drive the kids to her home because of severe storm

Last spoke Thursday morn. 2/19. Said she's being stalked by Bayside employee so both phone and email disabled according to her.

No word until Sat 2/21. Said she broke her arm Friday so couldn't call. Showed up at basketball game for Preston looking fine.

Week of 2/23 — All is fine. She begins her community

activities and seems hopeful. [Wynne had sought to join various advisory boards in San Francisco, such as the Opera Guild, with the help of friends.] She goes to L.A. for funeral midweek—misses L.B.'s [Little Britt's] birthday. Returns Friday 2/27.

Wednesday 3/4—Sounds slurry and drowsy

Thursday 3/5—Kids notice slurring

Friday 3/6—Britt lets her know that he senses something is wrong and states that he will not allow the kids to visit unless she agrees to a drug test. She refuses, becomes verbally abusive, still slurring. Many phone calls berating Britt well into the night. Britt still insisting on D & A [drug and alcohol] test & access to proof of program enrollment.

Saturday 3/7—Tells Preston she is filing emergency complaint because B. [Britt] won't allow kids to see her. Still slurring. Kids lose total faith.

Sunday 3/8—Double feature. [Wynne] says she wants kids for dinner, [ILLEGIBLE] when Britt maintains need for testing.

Monday 3/9—Several abusive phone calls to B.—heavy slur—many threats.

Monday 3/9—Says she has meeting with therapist & will have them call Britt to get records etc. No phone call.

Tuesday 3/10 — Heavy slurring. Several abusive phone calls. Making demands, threats, vulgarities.

Calls Little Britt a.m. saying she is making them dinner — Little Britt calls Britt, terrified — said Wynne told her she was going to serve lunch at school. Little Britt said she didn't sound like she'd make it.

Wynne accuses Britt of inflicting physical & emotional abuse on kids by not allowing them to see her.

Still refuses drug and alcohol test.

Demands Britt be tested — says it will be his fault when kids end up in foster care.

Preston calls Britt to say Wynne called for the first time in 2 weeks to complain about Britt. [ILLEGIBLE] told Wynne she was upset because Wynne hadn't called. Asked that she call at least once/week to report status.

Still refusing drug test.
Has left numerous messages
Preston confronted her on the phone.

Little Britt memory — Some apartment, watched Wynne fall in bathroom, dropped bottle of pills, scooped them up and put them all in her mouth. Seemed like a lot of pills to Little Britt.

Wednesday 3/11 — Not heard from until around 7:00 p.m.

All kids say they don't want to talk to her. Little Britt is afraid she'll show up to chaperone her field trip the next day. She calls repeatedly.

3/11 — Britt files for sole custody which is granted unless Wynne contests.

3/11 — Kids leave note thanking Britt for keeping them safe.

Calls Preston and Britt's phones during dinner. Preston very upset because he hates having to hang up on her. Britt tells her to stop calling.

Thursday 3/12 — She shows up at school. Berating school administration. They call Britt to help. He shows up & she yells and berates Britt. She leaves but parks 2 blocks away so Britt waits knowing that she will be back, which she is, and again he has to get her to leave before Little Britt sees the scene. Wynne threatens restraining order... leaves more nasty voicemails.

Friday 3/12 — Calls Britt, admits to being on morphine and Vicodin. Says her lawyer advised her not to tell him. Agrees to get herself together & not to call the kids until Britt says it's ok.

3/12 — She calls the house at 8 p.m. Little Britt and Harry don't want to answer the phone.

By week of 3/16 she seems manic all week. Preston confronts her again on the phone and in person. [Britt] feels like she might be doing better, and encourages the other two kids to talk with her.

Britt senses something is going on by Thursday. Starts making alternate plans for the kids for the weekend.

Foul-mouthed — vicious

Inappropriate bashing

Irresponsible decisions

The family is the most important to me

Little B. always has a sore throat

Harry baby talking

Putting fear into the kids

Verbally abusive to Preston

Not having regular clothes/supplies at her house

I'm afraid to be alone in the house sometimes — she is volatile and unpredictable.

More and more I choose to isolate and insulate

Little Britt and Harry tell me that they can keep her safe if they can be with her to make her happy

Is late for pick-ups, with no phone call.

Her dad threatening Preston

She got markedly meaner after the wedding

# Chapter 15

# Financial Ruin

## SOMETHING TO REMEMBER

*No matter who you are or what you're going through,*
*There's something you must remember to always do.*
*Surround yourself with people who care*
*Because believe it or not, there are many, I swear.*
*Remember that you're special and many love you.*
*There isn't anything that you can't get through.*
*You're strong and brave and unique in your own way.*
*There are people at your side to help you each day.*
*I know it may seem like your world is falling apart,*
*But remember that in life you have time for fresh starts.*

*Go out and see the world; travel to new places.*
*Be around fun and happy familiar faces.*
*Make mistakes and learn things you don't know.*
*This is the only way to ensure that you'll grow.*
*Use those curious eyes and that big great mind*
*To explore all of the happiness that's given to mankind.*
*Remember that this is only a piece of your wonderful life ahead,*
*So instead of looking down, try looking up instead.*

—K. BRITT DOYLE (Little Britt), age eleven

TRUTH AND I moved in together as we began our second year of dating. I felt so lucky that she considered me to be worth the chaos I brought to her life. We faced crisis after crisis over the next few years. The financial and emotional strain easily could have destroyed a first marriage, much less a blended family like ours. I couldn't have possibly foreseen the financial impact that my decisions would have on everyone in my family, both immediate and extended. I truly believed I could stage a comeback and "save" everyone, including Wynne.

Truth and I were married in September 2010 after spending two beautiful weeks together aboard a ship traveling up the Italian coast. Up until that trip, we had not been able to leave the Bay Area for any extended time, or for any real distance. Each time we left the kids with Wynne, something would happen and we'd need to scramble back or find someone to help. Being away for two full weeks and on the other side of the Atlantic Ocean was a huge stretch that gave us both anxiety as we left. We had several back-up plans in place, and Wynne's extended family of cousins, nieces, and nephews who were old enough to drive and to babysit were on standby. We had a truly wonderful ecosystem of people willing to make sure we had a worry-free vacation together. It worked.

Denny, Wynne's cousin and one of my closest friends, presided over the wedding. I can't remember feeling more alive. The guests were so enthusiastic and overjoyed to witness us as we made our vows. At the altar by my side were my two boys, Preston and Harry; Truth's son, Julian; my father; and Peter, our friend who had introduced us. At Truth's side were my daughter, Britt; Peter's wife, Catrina; and Zin, Leslie, Mandy, and Wendy, Truth's best friends in the world. It was the most fun I can remember. People were so happy for us.

We were still renting our home at this point. The instability I felt because of Wynne combined with capital losses from buying and selling homes in my past had made me skittish. My previous home-owning experiences also saw me investing considerable money, time, and sweat improving the grounds and interiors, only to feel my efforts were wasted because we soon sold the property. As a result, fixing up the house I lived in was no longer high on my long priority list. I regret that now because given everything she was doing for me and the kids, Truth deserved a place she could call a sanctuary. The house was definitely nice when we moved in together, but we did nothing to make it our own, even though we stayed there for over three years. We would eventually move twice more in Marin, still renting as my assets and cash flow continued to dwindle.

Standing on our balcony one night in early 2011 with a couple we had met recently at the tennis club, I was lamenting my decision to move to UBS to the husband, who had a background in finance as well. After spending several minutes discussing the downfall of the big banks during the 2008 crisis, he blurted out, "Let's start our own firm." He seemed very smart, and we'd hit it off fairly quickly, but I didn't really know him very well, so at first I downplayed his suggestion. Even though I still wasn't bringing home a paycheck, even after almost three years at UBS, the thought of leaving the "mother ship" seemed crazy. I had always told my friends at work how easy it would be to compete against an independent firm based just on the sheer size difference. How could a small independent firm succeed without access to the large array of products and services offered through the large banks? But his words took hold in my mind and I really began to consider the idea. Why not at least do a bit of due diligence and discovery? Even if I decided not to leave UBS, I would have a better knowledge of this segment of my competition. All it would cost me was time.

On Friday, October 28, 2011, at 4:55 p.m., I sat in my chair staring out at the Golden Gate Bridge. I had been working at UBS for just over three years. My desk was situated not five feet from the center of a floor-to-ceiling window that looked out on one of the most expansive and iconic structures in the world. I was about to give this up. My friend and I had decided to make a go of it. I was going further into debt every month, and the only way to stem the flow was to leave UBS. I had my resignation letter in my hand, along with the list of accounts I was going to contact, as required. I was the last person in the office that day. Those of us who were lucky enough to work in the private client markets on the West Coast worked on New York time. I'd left the office by 2:00 p.m. most Fridays since I began working at UBS, and now I found the late-afternoon silence almost overwhelming. I kept thinking someone I knew would walk through my door, and ask me what the hell I was doing there.

As I got up from my chair, I took a long look at my workspace to make sure I hadn't forgotten anything, then I turned off my computer monitors and pushed in my desk chair. I remember looking into each glass-walled office as I made my way down the corridor, almost hoping someone would be there. It felt like I was functioning inside a dream. My feet were like lead as I made my way past the last few offices before reaching my manager's empty desk. I knew this was the right decision for me, but it was also a decision I had been driven to out of necessity, given the hole I had dug myself into by optimistically believing that my book of business would follow me. Yet I was still holding out hope that I could fix my money problems. Optimism was my greatest asset in the face of total disaster. I had always been able to win when I put my mind to something.

The situation I was in now, though, was about to spin out of my control. I just didn't know that yet. UBS had lured me over with a hefty signing bonus, which I'd quickly used to pay off debt. When I left, they would try to claw it back—but I didn't have it.

I would end up fighting UBS for the next five years.

Chapter 16

# Coming Back
# to Life

*It's easy to be great when things are going well.*
*You find out who you are when things get tough.*

I WAS COMPLETELY BROKE, trying to maintain
two households, and recovering from a broken book of
business. I didn't bring home one paycheck in the three
years I was at UBS. That's not unusual in the financial

services world. The way it works is that a company entices high-earning advisors to jump firms by dangling huge signing bonuses in front of them. To make sure the new employees don't just pocket the money and then skip off to take another offer, they sign a contract that stipulates that the bonus represents a loan. Once they have met certain performance goals or been with the firm for a certain length of time, then the loan is forgiven. On the other hand, if the employee leaves before satisfying those conditions, they may be required to repay that money. Once the bonus is forgiven, the employee starts earning money.

This sort of deal is a common recruiting tool. I'd made the decision to use the proceeds of my signing bonus to pay down most of Wynne's and my debt, hoping to get out of that mess and give us both a fresh start.

We began our firm with high hopes. I was to bring large family accounts to the firm as I had successfully done for two decades at my previous jobs, and my partner was to bring large transactions with success fees attached, for what felt like the perfect combination for long-term growth and success. The only problem was that I didn't have the capital to sustain my living situation. I had always had a base from which to pay expenses—until now. But I still had confidence, as always, in my ability to raise capital, so I continued to borrow against what I thought were future earnings that were inevitable. This time, however, the loan came from my business partner's mother, collateralized by a significant stake in our firm.

Again, as my patterns began to show, I was making bad decisions—ones that focused on meeting my short-term needs but that would turn out to have long-term consequences. I didn't pay attention to the terms of the note because I had total faith in my ability to bring clients to our firm, and in my partner's desire to build a durable, stable, successful business together. We paid ourselves just enough to qualify for health care, and the rest of our earnings went to pay other salaries and expenses. I was trapped in my own self-created prison again, but at least this time I believed I had the ability to earn my way out quickly by building the new firm.

Not so fast.

As the business began to approach the size where we looked like we would be profitable, perhaps fifteen months into our journey, my partner exercised his right to assume his mother's loan to me and take a significant portion of my equity in the firm. It was that day that I completely lost all desire to continue to build that firm. His action, combined with another terrible choice I'd made, led to my departure from the firm.

That choice? I'd borrowed from a client. Even though the client had been a trusted friend for many years, borrowing money from clients is just not allowed in the wealth management field. I knew it was wrong when I did it, but I felt I had no choice at the time. That loan was crucial to save my family from the need to drastically change our lives; something I should not have been afraid of, looking back on it now. My family has proven to be significantly more resilient than I could have imagined or even hoped for.

But I didn't know that yet. Instead, I'd made what would become another in a long string of very poor financial decisions, each based on my belief that I had no other choice. For thirty-six months, I had continued to face a substantial monthly drain. I'd failed to bring my former clients over to UBS, and the ongoing fallout from the financial crisis of 2008 made it difficult to build up a new client list. I'd borrowed money in an attempt to stay afloat while I rebuilt my business again. I felt the only way out of *this* mess was to start my own firm where I could start earning right away, at least potentially, and hopefully negotiate with UBS for a long payback schedule for the bonus. In just a few short years, I had gone from being one of the most successful wealth management employees at Citigroup to being self-employed—which, in terms of money coming in, was no better than being unemployed. It wasn't that my fall was so painful (or maybe it was and I just couldn't admit it), but looking at the fear in Truth's eyes was my worst nightmare come true. I had failed the woman who believed in me blindly because I asked her to. She had walked into my life, which included three kids and a phenomenally chaotic situation with an ex-wife, and made me able to breathe again. There was no room for failure.

I had asked her to have faith in my ability to rebuild our lives in spite of the tremendous odds against being able to do it quickly enough. I truly believed I was capable of succeeding. I needed to be able to succeed, not only to be able to pay back my friends, who had believed in me too, but also for my own sense of self-worth. As I said before, my optimism was what gave me the ability to get up in the morning. On the other hand, it was also the root cause of my downfall as it clouded my ability to objectively assess my situation, which from the outside must have looked like a rocket ship reentering the atmosphere with no heat shields, breaking up as it burned across the sky until it fizzled out completely. One of my best friends said to me once that it was like I was running as fast as I could toward a cliff, hoping something or someone was going to stop me. Either way, I was going to be remembered.

Since I was little, I have always believed that I had a guardian angel. I believed that things happened for me just when I needed them most of my life. I do believe in God, but this is different. I'm not arrogant enough to think that God has his eye specifically on me, but I do believe there is a force that does. For the past few years, that guardian angel has been working overtime—but only if I let it.

I had recently met a man named Maxwell Drever while attending a conference in Los Angeles designed to educate families with significant assets about various investment strategies and best practices. A growing trend since the 2008 financial crisis has been very wealthy families taking their investments "in-house" by hiring a team dedicated to their affairs on a full-time

basis, thus eliminating sources of conflict in the financial services world that were illuminated during the
crisis. Maxwell was speaking about his investments in
multifamily apartment complexes for working families
around the country. While he was old enough to be my
father, Maxwell had a certain energy about him that
was contagious. He explained to the audience that you
could "do well by doing good," and that giving back
was his goal.

After his talk, I waited patiently in line to ask if I
could learn more about his fund so that I could present
it as an investment choice for my clients. We immediately hit it off, and began what would become a great
friendship.

While leaving the investment firm I had helped build
was extremely difficult on many levels, it has proved to
be one of the best things that I have done for myself.
I had not been careful in determining with whom and
how I wanted to build out the firm with my clients I had
been able to retain through the 2008 crisis.

After a few months trying to wrap my head around
the predicament I now found myself in, I called
Maxwell and asked to have dinner. As we sat down at
Don Antonio Trattoria in Tiburon, I began to outline

what I felt was a plan that would help the Drever family and team at his company, Drever Capital Management, integrate more heavily into the Family Office world. I didn't get more than five minutes into my pitch when he asked me point-blank what it would cost him. I immediately felt at ease. I loved his straightforward nature. He smiled as we agreed on a number, and I began a two-year stint working alongside one of the great men I have had the pleasure of knowing.

Not only was the work stimulating from the standpoint that Drever's company was really trying to make a difference, but my new office was located on his massive estate in Tiburon, right on the water. As we sat side by side in the office, waves crashing outside, I was overwhelmed with a sense of peace and hope that I had only felt a few times before, the last time being the day I met Truth.

For the next two years, from mid-2014 to mid-2016, I focused on meeting new families and groups interested in "impact investing"—choosing investments not only for financial gain but to make a measurable and positive social and environmental difference in the world. I needed this focus to maintain my optimism in the face of ultimately losing my battle with UBS. I knew

I was going to have to pay them back, but I was not prepared for the ferocity with which they came after me. It seemed as though they wanted to destroy any chance I had of financial recovery. I had been one of their star hires, so it makes sense that they would want to make an example out of me. They eventually won a claim not only for the remaining balance of the $3.66 million bonus I'd received after working three years of the required nine, but also another $1.5 million in interest and legal fees.

I wish things had been different. It's not like me to fail so spectacularly, and so publicly. It was difficult to hold my own head up, and no matter how much encouragement and guidance I tried to give Truth, I could tell she didn't want to leave the house. I couldn't blame her. How she stuck with me through this, I'll never know, but I'm grateful every day.

I went back to court to lower my alimony payments. They were cut in half, but that was still more than I was bringing in, and the judge was unsympathetic. My debt continued to grow as I borrowed more just to keep up with everything. I still felt that if I could only build back as quickly as I knew I was capable of, I could dig myself out without affecting the kids and Truth any more than I already had. They didn't deserve to suffer because of my flawed decisions. This was my battle that I knew I had to win.

During this period up to the beginning of 2015, Wynne was dividing her time between her apartment in San Francisco and her boyfriend's house in Santa Cruz. They had met at Narconon where he was working, and stayed together when she left. She appeared to be somewhat happy, but she always had the sense of desperation at having lost so much time with the kids, as well as the promise of the life she and I had started together twenty years earlier.

I recently saw a post one of my friends shared on Facebook that read: "The definition of Hell: The last day you have on earth, the person you became will meet the person you could have been." I guess that could apply to me as well. Although I couldn't be happier with the way my kids turned out after all of this, and I am madly in love with Truth, my career had been completely derailed because I chose to believe I could outrun the situation I was in rather than face it head on.

Chapter 17

# Overdose

### SHE SAID...

*She said everything would be good,*
*And she was doing all that she could.*
*I tried to do everything, everything I could do.*
*But she was telling lies, and she knew it too.*
*When times get tough, she turns to pills,*
*Not the good kind, but the kind that kills.*
*I see her lying there, shaking in her bed.*
*And there's nothing I can do but nod my head.*
*She falls down stairs, and breaks all her bones.*
*Then she calls my dad, and begs for loans.*

*There are so many memories, mainly bad . . .*
*And the thought of this makes me quite sad.*
*I wish there was a way I could make her see,*
*All she's doing to my brothers and me.*
*I see her cry and I hear her lie,*
*As I pray to God that time will go by.*
*But as time goes on, things stay the same.*
*And it's not my fault; I'm not to blame.*
*For it's all on her and the choices she made.*
*Now I sit here, thinking of what to do—*
*I need to save her, but I have not the slightest clue.*

—K. BRITT DOYLE (Little Britt), age twelve

THE KIDS WERE now working with a phenomenal therapy group with a focus on opiate and alcohol dependency called Recovery Without Walls in Mill Valley. It was Dr. Howard Kornfeld, the director of the facility, who was recently called on by the rock star Prince during the final few days of his life. Janis Phelps, one of the therapists there, was instrumental in developing the mindset the kids and Truth and I ultimately adopted about Wynne. I truly believe Janis was key in helping us reach and maintain mental health during the final few years of Wynne's life. We all accepted that we couldn't change her, and that she really didn't have a choice in how deep her disease went. She had never been able to voice the complete nature of her despair. Instead, she lashed out at everyone around her because she had no tools to communicate her pain and to own her actions. Janis brought a true sense of caring and love to the therapeutic process. As the kids grew older, she helped them to overcome guilt and confusion, trust in their own truths, find a measure of joy and forgiveness, and develop a positive sense of their own selves.

The week before she passed away, Wynne entered the hospital complaining of a large kidney stone that she said needed to be removed surgically. Her visits to the hospital had been so frequent over the years, it had become her second home. I figured this visit was just another way to get more pills, so I paid no attention. The kids were now driving, and were able to spend time with her on their own without me needing to constantly check in to make sure they were safe. The days passed with the kids making several visits to see her in the hospital. I never suspected anything, nor was I concerned that anything would go wrong. What I had not counted on, and didn't fully understand until months later, was that she was actually in withdrawal from the opiates she had been taking before she was admitted to the hospital. Normally, when she was admitted for a small surgical procedure (as had happened several times in the past), the stay was only a few days so she never exhibited extreme effects of withdrawal. She had become a master of covering that up over the years in order to appear sober and in good spirits for the kids as they got older and more sensitive to her actions.

Day 5 of her recommended 7-day hospital stay began with her adamantly telling the hospital staff that she needed to leave in order to see the kids because otherwise she would lose the visitation time she had been awarded for that week by the courts. I had always been an easy target for her to blame. Now, unbeknownst to me, she was telling her doctors that I was holding the kids from her. In truth, we had no set visitation schedule now; the kids were old enough to stay with her anytime they wanted, and I was all for them spending time with her, as Janis Phelps and we all agreed was best for everyone. Janis had always advocated that the kids try to spend time with Wynne in a nonjudgmental way to make sure that there would be no regrets when she ultimately passed away, which we all feared was a matter of time based on the amount of pills we knew she was taking.

Wynne had always had the ability to triangulate those around her by telling small lies that really could have been the truth given the way she told the story. Who wouldn't believe that an angry ex-husband could decide to hold the kids hostage from her or her family?

She left the hospital "AMA"—against medical advice—later that day, telling the medical staff she was being picked up by friends. In fact, she took a taxi to her home by herself. Believe it or not, the doctors and nurses who had been caring for her sent her home with seven prescriptions, including two for opiates, and one for benzodiazepines. Not only should they have known not to send any patient home with prescriptions for such a potentially deadly combination of drugs, but also they should have never given prescriptions to Wynne, who had been admitted to this hospital several times over the past fifteen years in varying states of overdosing. They must have had a file a mile thick on her with red letters saying "DO NOT GIVE OPIATES!"

Because she had been withdrawing for several days from the large doses of opiates she'd been taking before the kidney stone operation, she immediately filled the prescriptions and began trying to get her body back to the equilibrium she had been able to maintain for several years. This time, however, she was too weak, and the combination of high doses of opiates and benzodi-azepines at the same time caused her to stop breathing in the middle of the night.

Harry and Preston had driven over to her place to stay with her that night, and Harry had been there on the couch watching television as she stumbled into the bathroom for the last time, around 11:00 p.m. He had no idea that would be the last time he would see her alive. Nor did he think to help her at that moment because that was a state he had grown accustomed to seeing her in, especially at that time of the night.

The next morning, the boys and their friends who had spent the night there as well were leaving to work out. Preston yelled "good morning" to his mother through her closed door. No response. He knocked once, then twice, and uttered the same words. No response. He opened the door to find Wynne lying on her back, eyes wide open, staring blankly at the ceiling. Her hands were clenched behind her head with rigor mortis setting in so that her elbows stretched toward the ceiling. Preston ran to her immediately, trying to wake her up, but there was no sign of life, and her cold skin was turning a pale blue. He called 911, as I had done so many times in the past, and began chest compressions as the operator yelled through the phone for him to keep going until the paramedics got there. It was then that Harry called me. I could hear Preston in the background, crying and yelling to the operator that she was dead, and that he couldn't do any more to revive her. To this day, I can't imagine the horror Preston and Harry went through that morning, and the guilt they both harbor for having been there that night.

# Chapter 18

# Helping Others

## TRAPPED

*Lost, angry, confused, sad—*
*thinking of all the things she could have had.*
*Wishing that maybe she could find her way out—*
*but as her eyes filled with tears, her head filled with doubt.*
*Worthless, helpless, useless, stuck—*
*perhaps maybe this could just be bad luck?*
*But if that is true, and bad luck it was,*
*then why does she feel this awful kind of buzz?*
*"I'm fine," she'll say and we all know it's a lie,*
*for all she was thinking was when can I die?*
*Scared, lonely, invisible, sick—*

*waiting there alone as the clock goes tick.*
*As she then took the pills out of the drawer,*
*she felt her heart crumple, as it slowly tore.*
*And when someone came along, it was already too late.*
*She was already gone and there's no one to hate.*
*For she did this to herself because no one seemed to care.*
*Otherwise, maybe she wouldn't have breathed her last air.*

—K. BRITT DOYLE (Little Britt), age fifteen

HOW DO WE TURN this tragic ending into something positive? That was the question I asked my kids and myself once we got through the difficult period after Wynne's death and were able to collect ourselves. We all believed that the root cause of Wynne's behavior was her complete inability to talk about and own her issues. We had all tried to cover things up in one way or another at different times over the years. The deep shame and extreme guilt she felt over her loss of the family could be seen in the wall collage she had put together in her apartment years earlier. We needed to take our personal experience, and try to make sense of it so that others might know that they're not alone. One conversation might start an avalanche of others, and maybe we could help end this epidemic.

Preston, Harry, and Britt now felt free to tell me stories they'd kept secret before out of fear that I would hold them back from seeing their mother. For the most part the stories were awkward, because the kids wanted to tell them in a way that made them somewhat funny and yet it was impossible to miss the undertone of distress, either theirs or their mother's. While many of these stories described how she interacted with them or other people they came in contact with, others involved instances where damage was done to a car or to her apartment due to impairment on her part. Of course I was hesitant to let them see her during times I knew she was under the influence, but as the kids grew older and more confident, I gave them more control over their own decisions about when they wanted to see her. And yet, they still felt the need to hide things from me regarding their mother's substance abuse, fearing what my reaction would be.

I started writing down my own memories and thoughts, going all the way back to the beginning. After several months and many pages, I looked back on what I had written and realized how visceral and bitter it was. Writing was cathartic in a way as for the first time I was able to express my feelings about the things Wynne had done, and about the circumstances that led to her death.

I combed the Internet looking for organizations that I felt understood my experiences, and had the same mindset regarding the shame and guilt I had observed in our small family ecosystem. When I found the Shatterproof website, I felt instantly that Gary Mendell, its founder, absolutely got it. I picked up the phone and called him directly. After twenty minutes of explaining our story, and listening to how Gary was not only building an organization to tackle the stigma and shame of addiction, but also devoting his own time and resources to changing the laws governing opioid prescription-writing on a state-by-state basis, I was hooked. I wasn't sure how I could possibly help, but after several more discussions with him and his staff, I was excited about becoming one of the first Shatterproof Ambassadors, a group of volunteer peer leaders trained to share our stories and help others in our respective communities understand the magnitude of the opioid epidemic. We needed to get people talking.

Gary announced that he and other Shatterproof staff members were going to attend the CDC hearings on developing national guidelines for prescribing opioids that were going to be held in January 2016. I wasn't able to attend the hearings in person, but call-in numbers allowed those of us with stories and opinions to participate.

Listening to the statistics about the ongoing national epidemic was an extraordinary experience for me. It was the first time I understood that my family's painful story was part of something much larger. I heard many stories that were similar to mine, but I seemed to be the only one whose situation had ended in the death of a mother with three kids. Jeanne Whalen, a reporter for the *Wall Street Journal*, soon contacted me to ask for more detail. Her article, "Families Press CDC for Painkiller Prescription Guidelines," featured both my story and Gary's, and appeared in the paper on January 29. Shortly thereafter, HBO contacted us both to participate in a documentary they were producing to illuminate how this epidemic was affecting different families in different ways. Little did I know how articulate and thoughtful my kids would sound during their sequences. I had been successful in one aspect of this crisis, no doubt. The stories they told of their mother as they grew up with her addiction were delivered in such a way that you could tell they not only loved her, but certainly forgave her completely. Our internal family dynamic that allowed us to speak openly and develop a strong respect for one another proved to be a very powerful tool in the battle we fought.

Feeling that there was much more that I could be doing, a few months later I decided to join the Alcohol and Drug Advisory Board to the Marin County Board of Supervisors. We advise the Board of Supervisors on policies and goals of treatment programs, educate the public about alcohol and drug problems, network with other community resources, and encourage support throughout Marin County for development and implementation of effective alcohol and drug programs.

Most of all, though, it's a way for me to show the kids that we care as a family, and to model that when we have an extraordinary insight into something that we might be able to help with, we do it. Since joining, the kids and I have spoken in front of large groups, and spent time writing about our family story. I'm encouraged by their grace and poise when they discuss their experiences with others. The subject of how others treated their mother, both good and bad, is often what gets them motivated. They learned some valuable skills through Recovery Without Walls, and by talking with each other over the years. That's their gift to us and to themselves. They have proven the value of nonjudgmental love, relationships that value communication, and the beauty of embracing the shame others feel. Watching them articulate all this is their greatest gift to me.

On the financial side, the decisions I made to keep up with the ever-increasing chaos while Wynne was alive were obviously not wise. I acted like an addict myself in an odd way; I was frantic to keep things stable while making choices that would ultimately harm me and my family. Armed with the belief that I was capable of building my business back quickly because I had done it twice before—once when I was just beginning my career, and again after the tech market crash in 2000—I borrowed money from anyone I could to bridge the gap, or as my father described it, "kick the can down the road." I believed with all my heart that I was going to be able to repay the debts I had to good friends. I still believe that—I simply had to take control of my life, and make some hard choices.

I can tell you that I have a much greater appreciation now for the amount of work it takes to put one's financial life back together after it falls apart, and as a result, I am far more fiscally conservative than I ever was before. It's been such a struggle to hold everything together. I will never forget what it feels like to wonder how I was going to come up with rent in just a few days. The shame at losing control of my client base, and ultimately my confidence in myself, has definitely taken a toll, but looking at it in a positive light, I have been given a real gift. Not only do I know who my true friends are, I have a greater appreciation for trust, loyalty, and character. I will never take what I have for granted again.

In my professional life, I have been blessed with the opportunity to meet several terrific people who had confidence in me even when I didn't have confidence in myself. Two in particular, Pam Krueger and Jeff Heely, have given me a clear path to follow for the future. Pam and I have worked very closely for the past year building her company, WealthRamp, which introduces individuals and families to independent fiduciary wealth advisors and their firms using an algorithm based on questions they answer. I'm grateful for the opportunity to help build such a necessary tool in this finance space.

Recently, Jeff asked me to join him in building out an infrastructure private equity fund with Witt Global Partners. Not only is it exciting and necessary work as

well, but also it feeds directly into my strength in connecting families and their desire to invest in projects
that produce great returns *and* have the potential to
make a difference. We are working out of Little Rock,
Arkansas, where the company founder, former White
House Cabinet Member James Lee Witt, has assembled an amazing team of high achievers. Each of us
has terrific respect for what the others in the group have
already accomplished in their lives. For the first time
in my work life, I feel like I am in the right place at
the right time. I am breathing again, and I am deeply
appreciative of those people in my life who have kept
me going. I look forward to the next chapter.

# Chapter 19

# Through the Eyes of the Children

## WHERE DID YOU GO?

*I miss you, Mama.*
*Where did you go?*
*There are so many things I wish you could know.*

*My head is spinning and my body aches.*
*I think of you and my entire heart breaks.*
*I wake up each day in hope that you're there.*
*But as the days go on, I see you're nowhere.*

*People tell me that I should feel you right here,*
*But you feel so far away and you never appear.*
*I am completely helpless and have no idea what to do.*
*I need you back in my life, if only you knew.*

*You're my best friend and the most special person I know.*
*I hate that you won't be here to watch me as I grow.*
*What happens to the plans that we promised to make?*
*Like all of the fun trips that we were supposed to take.*

*I can't do this alone; I need you at my side.*
*I thought it was you and me on this crazy ride.*
*I understand that life is filled with surprises and pain,*
*But the thought of not having you is making me insane.*

*My world is crushed and nothing seems right;*
*It's like going through a tunnel without any light.*
*It's hopeless and disappointing because the pain won't end . . .*
*I doubt that I'll ever actually fully comprehend.*

*Losing you is most definitely the worst thing ever,*
*But please never forget that my love for you will remain forever.*

—K. Britt Doyle (Little Britt), age sixteen

Wynne's struggle with addiction was not just hers alone. It challenged everyone around her, especially our children. As I was writing this book, I asked the kids if they would like to add anything. Little Britt offered to share her poems, written over a span of seven years during some of the lowest times in her mother's life. Preston and Harry chose to write the following words, which I'm honored to include here.

## Preston

Growing up with my mother has been both the greatest privilege and struggle of my life. Often consumed in the daily routine, the role of a mother is overlooked. The job is the job; she's Mom, and there's no changing that.

In her short time here, Mom was always the enthusiastic, sarcastic, and adventurous woman I was proud to show my friends. She truly made my happiness her mission. Whatever I wanted, I knew she would do anything to see it happen. I always knew how loving and affectionate she was and almost took that for granted. So the real question is: why would any person give a happy and seemingly stable life to prescription drugs?

What took me the longest time to understand is that people generally embody the person they want you to see. My mom was someone I indirectly modeled my temperament and personality after, so I guess the real question is: what was she hiding? Her prescription drug abuse was brought into the light by my father at an early age, and I appreciate the clarity that brought to so many previously unexplained phenomena in regard to her tendencies. I knew from age ten of her affliction and saw no other option but to confront and deal with the problem head on. She'll stop if her preteen son has the guts to confront and acknowledge such a delicate situation, right? What I found over the years is that her prescription drug abuse served to fill some unspoken void. We as a family could only guess the origin, as no acknowledgement would come from her, so it's unfair to expect cooperation on such introspective probing. There's obviously a reason she's hiding the root of such pain and mental anguish so deeply.

Year after year, from that point, we would go through the same routine; we would spend as much time with her as possible and enjoy every second of it. The cynical part of me silenced my aggressive attitude toward her addiction and learned not to take her habits so personally. Relapses would come and go, and a new affection and appreciation for my mom replaced my anger. I began to see all the sacrifices she made and would make for the happiness of me and my siblings.

I also began to see that her problem was bigger than all of us and our trajectory was seemingly set. A new perspective was due before that day would come; the day I always expected, yet pushed aside. I can honestly say that I spent the last few years of her time on this planet in a frame of mind that truly allowed our connection to flourish. There's no reason to say that an ending like this is inevitable, but why not look at the situation for what it really is? My mother had an issue, an issue in which I had no influence, so what right do I have to judge? I will always love her, I am bitter to have lost her, but I am undeniably lucky to have called her my mother.

## Harry

It is noon on Saturday, March 21, 2015. I'm home alone with Mom. She has just gotten back from the hospital for a kidney stone. She tells me that she is having trouble breathing, and jokingly I say, "Sucks for you." The smirk on her face lets me know that she is pretty cool. She sends me out with forty dollars to get a prescription from Walgreens and when I return, she immediately takes three puffs from the inhaler in the bag. When I see that the inhaler isn't working for her, I ask how she feels. She tells me that it takes a while to kick in, but I know that is false because I used to use one when I was younger. I then tell her that if her breathing continues to bother her, I would go back to Walgreens. She chuckles and tells me that she'll be fine.

I then let my four friends into the front of the apartment and introduce them to her. One by one, they say hello as she sits up in her bed. The five of us then head downtown to Union Square for the rest of the day. Around 9:00 p.m., I return home to find her asleep. I tiptoe past her bedroom and turn on the TV to watch Comedy Central. My last memory of her that night is around 10:30 p.m., when she gets some food and heads back to her room to go to sleep.

Everyone loses their parents but it's different when you are sixteen and watch it happen over your entire life to that point. I found out on a Sunday morning in March that I had lost my mother sometime during the night after her fifteen-year frantic battle with opiate addiction. The best advice I was given was to love her unconditionally, and cherish every moment until she was gone. I learned compassion and how to find the good in an otherwise hopeless situation. All around her, people shook their heads, wondering why she wouldn't stop, but our relationship was unequivocal and nonjudgmental.

Since her passing, there hasn't been a day that goes by that she isn't in my thoughts and influencing my decisions. Many nights I return to the neighborhood where she lived, the Embarcadero in San Francisco, to ride my skateboard as I did before. The freedom I feel skating down her old street at night, by myself, is when I feel most alive. I sat in on a homeless rally one night, listening to people with seemingly nothing talk about the beautiful world we live in. It was a moment that truly inspired me.

I believe people do the best they can with what they have. The shame and stigma of addiction can be overwhelming for some, but I know from my own experience that compassion and love allow those left behind to remember the positive.

# Life Lessons

OVER THE COURSE of writing this book, I've thought a lot about my life. Nothing can change the past. All I can do now is try to learn from what happened, and then consciously try to apply what I've learned when I face difficult choices and decisions in the future.

Work toward greater control over things we do have control over, and let go of those things we have no control over. Set boundaries—not only for the substance abuser, but also for yourself and your family—around how you interact with that person, and how you take care of yourself.

We need other people. Learn to reach out to others so you can receive help and give support. This is a tough lesson to learn but it can serve us in all aspects of our lives.

There is a reason things get out of control in the first place. Find that root cause and work on that.

Our intentions and deeds add up to patterns and a way of life. Be present always, and strive to lead the life you deserve without shame and guilt.

Self-care is paramount. Substance abuse can produce so much chaos that you may find yourself racing from one likely disaster to the next, neglecting the physical, emotional, social, and spiritual needs of yourself and those you love.

There is no "one size fits all" diagnosis or reason for substance abuse. It could be affected by genetics, home environment, personal trauma, mental disorders, lack of coping mechanisms, or a combination of those things.

A person's struggle is not their identity. The substance abuser is not lazy or lacking motivation. Do not shame those struggling. Everyone has their own battles and demons they're fighting on a daily basis.

Bad decisions are a slippery slope. Compromise leads to more compromise, no matter what the subject in question.

# Acknowledgements

I WANT TO acknowledge many people who have touched my life in a positive way and pushed me to finish this book. First, even though the stories and consequences are still so raw, I want to thank Truth and my kids for their respect and love while I wrote the book. Thank you to my mother, father, and brother for always keeping the door open and the light on when I needed a break. Thanks to Brannon Beliso and Dennis Chiodo for being at the right place at the right time and for giving me perspective I was unable to find by myself. Thank you to my friend Martin Connolly for always being there, even in the darkest moments. Thank you to my Aunt Susie and my cousin Samara for calming me down every time I thought the world was ending. Thank you to my friend Tom McCarthy, who moved my family seven times in the past eleven years.

Finally, thank you to Jennifer Weiksner, Susan Shankin, and Ruth Mullen for taking what was in my head and making it so much better.

# Bibliography

"Health Care Costs from Opioid Abuse: A State-by-State Analysis." Partnership for Drug Free Kids. April 2015. http://drugfree.org/wp-content /uploads/2015/04/Matrix_OpioidAbuse_040415 .pdf

"Increases in Drug and Opioid Overdose Deaths— United States, 2000–2014." *Morbidity and Mortality Weekly Reports*, Centers for Disease Control and Prevention. January 01, 2016. https://www.cdc .gov/mmwr/preview/mmwrhtml/mm6450a3 .htm?s_cid=mm6450a3_w

"Jail Becomes Home for Husband Stuck With Lifetime Alimony." Bloomberg.com. August 27, 2013.
https://www.bloomberg.com/news
/articles/2013-08-26/jail-becomes-home-for
-husband-stuck-with-lifetime-alimony

"Number and Age-adjusted Rates of Drug-poisoning
Deaths Involving Opioid Analgesics and Heroin:
United States, 2000-2014." National Vital Statistics
System, Mortality File, Centers for Disease Control
and Prevention. December 9, 2015. https://www
.cdc.gov/nchs/data/health_policy/AADR_drug
_poisoning_involving_OA_Heroin_US_2000-2014

"Opioid Painkiller Prescribing Varies Widely among
States." Press release prepared for U.S. Department of Health and Human Services. Centers for
Disease Control and Prevention. July 01, 2014.
https://www.cdc.gov/media/releases/2014
/p0701-opioid-painkiller.html

"Prescription Opioid Use Is a Risk Factor for Heroin Use," *Prescription Opioids and Heroin.* National Institute on Drug Abuse, National Institute of Health. 2015. https://www.drugabuse.gov/publications /research-reports/relationship-between-prescription -drug-heroin-abuse/prescription-opioid-use-risk -factor-heroin-use

Whalen, Jeanne. "Families Press CDC for Painkiller Prescription Guidelines." *The Wall Street Journal.* January 28, 2016. https://www.wsj.com/articles /families-press-cdc-for-painkiller-prescription -guidelines-1454023695

# Resources

## Alcohol Justice

(www.alcoholjustice.org): Promotes evidence-based public health policies and organizes campaigns with diverse communities and youth against the alcohol industry's harmful practices

## Bereaved Parents of the USA

(www.bereavedparentsusa.org): Offers support, understanding, encouragement, and hope to fellow bereaved parents, siblings, and grandparents after the death of their loved one

**Community Anti-Drug Coalitions of America**
(www.cadca.org): Premier membership organization
representing those working to make their communities
safe, healthy, and drug-free

**Coping with Grief: How to Handle Your
Emotions** (www.everydayhealth.com/healthy-living
/coping-with-grief.aspx): Article from the Everyday
Health website

**Dealing with the Anniversary of a Loved One's
Death** (www.whatsyourgrief.com/dealing-with-the
-anniversary-of-a-loved-ones-death): Article from the
What's Your Grief website

**HelpGuide's Coping with Grief and Loss**
(www.helpguide.org/articles/grief-loss/coping-with
-grief-and-loss.htm): Article from the Helpguide
website

**How to Cope with Loss**
(www.wikihow.com/Cope-With-Grief): Article from
the Wikihow website

**Partnership for Drug-Free Kids**
(www.drugfree.org): Committed to helping families struggling with their son or daughter's substance

use; empowers families with information, support, and guidance to get the help their loved one needs and deserves; advocates for greater understanding and more effective programs to treat the disease of addiction

## RX Safe Marin

(www.rxsafemarin.org): Coalition of community members and experts collaborating to tackle the local prescription drug misuse and abuse epidemic

## Shatterproof

(www.shatterproof.org): Committed to ending the stigma of addiction and helping those with this disease fully recover

## Ten Ways to Support Someone After a Death From Drugs in Their Family (www.verywell.com /support-after-death-from-drugs-22137): Article from the VeryWell website

## STRONGER THAN ADDICTION

## Shatterproof Encourages Strengthening Reporting Requirements For Cures Database

**Opioid overprescribing is directly contributing to America's addiction crisis.**

- The number of opioid painkillers prescribed and sold in the United States increased four times between 1999 and 2014.

- In that same time period, the number of opioid-related deaths increased almost five times.

**It's an especially big problem here in California.**

- In 2014, California had the largest number of over-dose deaths of any state in the nation.

- California's hospitals treat an opioid or heroin over-dose about every 25 minutes.

- In states like California that do not have legislative mandates, **86% of opioid prescriptions are written without ever checking the patient's prescription history.**

**Prescription Drug Monitoring Programs are a proven, common-sense solution.**

- PDMPs are state-run electronic databases that collect information about controlled substance prescriptions from in-state pharmacies. They are among the most promising state-level interventions to improve painkiller prescribing, inform clinical practice, and protect patients at risk.

- "Doctor shoppers" are 7 times more likely to die of an opioid overdose, and people who have concurrent prescriptions of benzodiazepines and opioids are 4 times more likely to die of an overdose. PDMPs help identify and protect these individuals.

**States with mandatory PDMP querying see lower levels of opioid prescribing. Take New York, for example.**

- In 2013, New York passed legislation consistent with the recommendations being proposed here in California. In the first year, doctor shopping decreased 75%, the number of opioid doses dispensed decreased by 10%, and the number of prescriptions for buprenorphine, a drug used to treat opioid addiction, increased by 15%. Similar results have been achieved in several other states.

**PDMP legislation is making progress in California.**

Senator Lara (D-Los Angeles) has taken leadership on this issue and introduced legislation that would require physician PDMP reporting. The bill SB482:

- Mandates that every prescriber consult the PDMP before prescribing a Schedule II or III controlled substance for the first time, and then again annually if the substance remains a part of the patient's treatment

- Stipulates that failure to comply is subject to disciplinary action by the appropriate licensing board

**Shatterproof recommends that the bill should also include these expert-recommended requirements:**

- Expand mandatory query requirements to include Schedule IV substances, too

- Require prescribers to query the system upon every prescription, rather than just annually

- Require pharmacists to submit prescription information to the PDMP within 24 hours of dispensing the medication (currently, pharmacists in California have 7 days to do this)

- Publish findings on statewide opioid overdose data, so we can always be looking for ways to further reduce overdoses

**Shatterproof strongly supports life-saving PDMP legislation. Join our advocacy efforts and make your voice heard now.**

Text "Shatterproof" to 52886, or visit takeaction.shatterproof.org/CA to get involved today.

# About the Author

BRITT DOYLE IS a thirty-year veteran of the Capital Markets, having started his career as an institutional fixed income salesman for Security Pacific Asian Bank in Singapore directly out of college. After receiving an MBA in the late 1980s, he moved to the private client side of the business, working for various large investment banks, including Kidder Peabody, Merrill Lynch, and UBS. Most of his career, however, was spent as a member of Citigroup's elite Family Office division, where he developed the knowledge and skillset necessary to work with ultra-wealthy families on a variety of relevant topics.

At Witt Global Partners, Britt's responsibilities will include sourcing and vetting alternative asset funds, and direct capital raises within the Family Office and Independent Wealth Advisor channel.

Britt graduated with a BA in Asian Studies from the University of California, Berkeley, and received an MBA from the University of Southern California, where he served as a founding member of the Student Investment Fund. Britt is an avid tennis player and former children's kenpo karate instructor. He is an Ambassador for Shatterproof, a national organization committed to protecting children from addiction to alcohol and other drugs, and also serves on the Alcohol and Other Drug (AOD) Advisory Board to the Marin County Board of Supervisors.

He lives with his wife and four children in Marin, California.

**Britt's thoughts about being profiled in the HBO Documentary:**
*Warning: This Drug May Kill You*

Perri Peltz and her team at HBO have put the spotlight squarely on a drug epidemic unlike any seen before in our country—unlike the others, this one started in the doctor's office. During the course of working with the filmmakers, I gained new understanding of the causes and the devastating nature of long-term opiate use, even though I'd already lived it. Many people have some understanding of the issues, but only once we all start communicating and telling our stories will we be able to form a full picture of this situation.

Help get the message of this book out to others:
please share it on Facebook, Twitter, and other social media.

We'd also appreciate your review of it on amazon.com
or other book review websites.